After Some Time

Connecting with *Women* through Real-Life Stories

Solé Wright

SUGAR MAPLE BOOKS

Copyright ©2023 by Solé Wright
Published by Sugar Maple Books

All rights reserved.

No portion of this book may be reproduced in any form without written permission from the publisher or author, except as permitted by U.S. copyright law.

This publication is designed to provide accurate and authoritative information in regard to the subject matter covered. It is sold with the understanding that neither the author nor the publisher is engaged in rendering legal, or other professional services. While the publisher and author have used their best efforts in preparing this book, they make no representations or warranties with respect to the accuracy or completeness of the contents of this book and specifically disclaim any implied warranties of merchantability or fitness for a particular purpose. No warranty may be created or extended by sales representatives or written sales materials. The advice and strategies contained herein may not be suitable for your situation. You should consult with a professional when appropriate. Neither the publisher nor the author shall be liable for any loss of profit or any other commercial damages, including but not limited to special, incidental, consequential, personal, or other damages.

Scripture quotations taken from The Holy Bible, New International Version®, NIV® ©1973, 1978, 1984, 2011 By Biblica, Inc.
Used with permission. All right reserved worldwide.

1st edition 2023 Revised

ISBN: 979-8-9887676-0-2 (pbk)
ISBN: 979-8-9887676-1-9 (ebook)

" ... to the only wise God be glory forever through Jesus Christ! Amen." (Romans 16:27)

I dedicate this book to the loving memory of my mother. The spirit of her perseverance and faith lives in me and my children.

To the women who have confided in me and shown incredible strength in the face of life's storms. We are in this together.

To you, dear reader, may you not only find yourself within these chapters, but connect with Jesus—the lover of your soul.

Contents

Introduction	VII
1. Set The Stage	1
2. Seeking	25
3. Identity	47
4. Secrets	73
5. Hard Times	95
6. Religion or Relationship	119
7. A New Life	141
8. Surrender	163
Epilogue	188
A Note From Me	196

Acknowledgements	198
Resources	200
Endnotes	202
About The Author	204

Introduction

"May these words of my mouth and this meditation of my heart be pleasing in your sight, Lord, my Rock and my Redeemer." (Psalms 19:14)

HOPING TO AVOID ANYONE I knew, I rushed towards the checkout lane. I didn't want to recount the details of *that day* to someone else—the reason for my limp. I longed for things to return to normal, but knew the person I once was no longer existed. Life is different now. I am different.

While checking out, I recognized the woman behind me. She was a woman I looked up to as a mentor while raising my children. If it had been another person, I would have pretended not to notice her—my exhaustion was that overwhelming.

However, her friendly face and love for her caught me off guard and I blurted out her name "Patricia!" My spirit fluttered with joy as I remembered what this friendship meant to me. We exchanged the common pleasantries of *hello, nice to see you, hope you are doing well* and it was my turn to check-out.

As I was about to pay, Patricia slipped me a pen and paper and asked for my phone number. I wrote my number on the paper and gave it to her. Before we said our goodbyes, we threw the final *let's have coffee and get caught up* pitch. I wanted to catch up, but didn't think it would actually happen. How often do we suggest a coffee date with a friend and don't follow up? It's not that we don't want to, but our busy schedules prevent us from making time for *one more thing*.

A week later, Patricia called, and we scheduled our date. During this season of brokenness, I was particular about who I surrounded myself with. I knew Patricia to be a safe person. She was full of wisdom and I could trust her if my tears joined our conversation.

Patricia told me she had been thinking about me. She didn't know about my struggles, yet the Holy Spirit had prompted her to pray for me. Have you ever thought of someone and, out of the blue, you run into them? Follow-up with them. There is something in that *running into* that God wants to bring to your attention.

Even though it had been about 15 years since we last had a meaningful visit, we connected again as if there was no gap in time. We shared where we were in life and found common ground in our conversations. Patricia's words provided comfort by resonating to a similar life experience as I was going through. Her story gave me hope, knowing that this suffering will not last forever; redemption will come *after some time*. During our conversation, my words reassured her that God was speaking in a specific area and gave her the green light to proceed. This is the picture of iron sharpening iron (Proverbs 27:17).

This often happens when women gather—we edify and affirm each other. That morning I walked into the coffee shop feeling dull, but left sharp as a blade! God had been waiting for both of us there—all we had to do was show up to receive His blessings.

Before diving into this book, I recommend having a friend join you on this journey. Knowing you are not alone nurtures the healing process, and listening to others' stories helps you navigate your own. We need each other.

Throughout this book, you will get to know me through short stories, such as I would share with a trusted friend over coffee. Although the short stories are mostly about me, this book is intended for you to explore your own life experiences as well. It's also about experiencing God's redemption, through Jesus, for your life.

As you read, find the common ground, the emotional connections, and take the time to *unpack* the parts of your story that come to mind. Write down the thoughts and memories that emerge. Resist the urge to continue reading until you have read the suggested Scripture verse(s) and answered the *Pause and Reflect* questions. These exercises are a part of the redemptive process and will enable you to enter your story and allow room for healing.

Each chapter ends with a redemptive story of a difficult season of my life, my *After Some Time*. I pray that your soul is stirred, encouraging you to examine areas in your life where you may be stuck.

Twenty years ago, God put a desire in my heart to write my redemptive story. I wrote a little here and there, but for my eyes only. I was most comfortable with personal journaling. Journaling is a practice I have been doing since I was young. It served as a release from negative thoughts.

When I became a Christian, my journaling evolved. It included prayers and notes from my daily Bible readings. All throughout this journey, I have sought God's will for my life; *seeking doesn't always mean doing*. This consistent seeking reaped a personal relationship and reliance on Him. Even in my intimate relationship with God, daily reading of the Word, journaling and seeking His will, I still found myself trapped by childhood lies that said:

Something is wrong with me.

After all these years, it came down to a secret I kept. I believed the lie that no one would understand. I couldn't explain this secret because it was difficult to figure out that part of my story. I spent most of my life stuck as a captive to the greater lie that I was alone in this specific situation. I share my story to encourage you to expose the secrets that are holding you back and to let go of the belief that you are alone.

"What has been will be again, what has been done will be done again; there is nothing new under the sun." (Ecclesiastes 1:9)

Please understand that I am not trying to downplay your pain or experiences. The challenges that some women have overcome are beyond my comprehension. I want nothing more than to express how sorry I am that you have suffered at the hands of someone's carelessness or evil actions. As I write this, I feel a heaviness, an aching in my heart, thinking about the stories women have shared with me. Their stories have confirmed to me that we are all connected through pain and suffering. I pray the stories in this book offer you hope and give you a glimpse of God's redemptive nature.

In my adult life, God began redeeming parts of my childhood story before I even realized it. His first and greatest act of redemption was giving His one and only Son, Jesus Christ, to pay for my wrongs, my sins.

The definition for the word 'redeemed' in the Merriam-Webster dictionary is:

1. *a: to buy back: REPURCHASE*
   b: to get or win back

2. *: to free from what distresses or harms: such as*
   a: to free from captivity by payment of ransom
   b: to extricate from or help to overcome something detrimental
   c: to release from blame or debt: CLEAR
   d: to free from the consequences of sin

3. *:to change for the better:* REFORM

4. *:* REPAIR, RESTORE[1]

I don't know about you, but I want all of that!

One of my favorite redemptive stories is in the Old Testament found in 2 Samuel 4. The story introduces Mephibosheth, a young boy who became lame in both feet at the tender age of five. His caretaker was fleeing with him from imminent danger when "he fell and became disabled" (v. 4). Mephibosheth did nothing to deserve this injury. *It was not his fault.*

I wonder if this disability isolated him, keeping him from running around with his friends. Maybe he felt insecure over his limp, or as if he wasn't enough because he was broken. Perhaps as he got older, he didn't dream big dreams for himself because of his limitations.

Maybe you are like Mephibosheth. You did nothing to deserve what happened to you. Someone neglected to protect you and you have suffered an injury, and like Mephibosheth, you have been walking with a limp ever since. Perhaps your focus has remained on your injury and not on the One who longs to heal you.

Maybe it wasn't so much that he was lame, but there was a fear that whatever they were running from would come back for him. Mephibosheth was being protected from the poor choices his grandfather Saul made. This had nothing to do with this little boy, yet it affected him. The consequences of our ancestors' choices, whether good or bad, can affect us.

Are you aware of generational sins within your family? Have you noticed recurring negative patterns in yourself or family members, like suicide, infidelity, fear, addiction, greed, abortion, divorce, anger, or pride? You will notice how these patterns emerge in our lives through my mother's story and mine causing harm, just like with Mephibosheth.

In 2 Samuel 9, we read more of his story. David asked, "Is there anyone still left of the house of Saul to whom I can show kindness, for Jonathan's sake?" This is when Mephibosheth comes back on the scene. We read in verse 12 that he had a young son. He learned to do life with his injury. It's something we all do. We learn to *get by*, but are we thriving?

King David told him, "I will surely show you kindness for the sake of your father Jonathan. I will restore to you all the land that belonged to your grandfather Saul, and you will always eat at my table" (v. 7).

The land where he fled from was being returned to him, yet his reply was, "What is your servant, that you should notice a dead dog like me" (v. 8)? Okay, this has shame written all over it. *No, King David, I don't deserve this. Don't you know where I came from, who my granddaddy is? Don't you realize I am lame, worthless? I have nothing to offer you.* I can identify with Mephibosheth's response to King David's generosity. The voice of shame always drowns out the truth of who we are.

What can I possibly offer?
If people knew ...

How often have we let the shame from our past hinder us from receiving God's blessing?

Here's where the story gets good. King David ignored his reply and immediately summoned Saul's steward to restore Mephibosheth to everything that belonged to Saul (v. 9). What's even better, the king invited Mephibosheth to eat at his table as one of his own sons (v. 11).

Oh, the beauty of redemption! What a beautiful story and future hope for us, as one day we will sit at the King's table. The King of Kings has already redeemed us and one day we will dine with him.

> God is saying, *Come to me so I can restore what has been taken from you. Walk with me and I will show you the plans I have for your life. Let us eat together every day and get to know me as your REDEEMER.*

Let me tell you, redemption happens *after some time*. I love those words! *After some time*, I learned to forgive my offenders. *After some time*, I began to love myself the way God designed me. *After some time*, I saw what hurt me turned into my life's purpose.

Redemption is available to all, no exceptions. The best news I have for you right now is that your story is still unfolding. My prayer for you is that God will reveal the negative patterns in your life, and those secrets that are keeping you from experiencing all that He has planned for you (Jeremiah 29:11-14).

This is my redemptive journey as it continues to unfold.

After some time ... what will your redemption story be?

The following stories are based on my point of view. These are my memories, experiences, and perspectives. I can't remember what age I was during certain events in my childhood. The ages I have written are what I believe to be accurate. Out of respect and privacy, I have changed names and identifiers in the stories and people in this book.

1
Set The Stage

You, Lord, took up my case; you redeemed my life.
(Lamentations 3:58)

Meet Mom

NOTIFICATIONS WERE POURING IN when I turned my phone on. While making my way to the center aisle of the airplane, I listened to the first message. It was my sister-in-law, Monica, with news that punched me in the gut. Before I could retrieve my bag from the overhead compartment, my legs collapsed, causing me to fall back onto my seat. The man behind me asked if I was alright. I could not say it—*Mom just died*.

I was hurrying from Michigan to Florida to get a handle on her health and to persuade her to come and live with me. The night before, my older brother Alex had called. "Something is not right with mom. Could you call her? See what you can find out." I got off the phone with him and called her.

Mom had been recovering from a stroke in a care home before being transferred to the hospital. The nurse answered the phone.

"Hi, This is Solé, Sara's daughter. Is there a chance I can speak with her?"

"She has been unresponsive for most of the day." The nurse informed me.

"Can you please put the phone to her ear?" I asked, hoping my voice would elicit a reaction from mom.

Spanish was my first language, and that's mostly what I spoke to mom in. However, as I got older, it became what some of us call Spanglish—a mix of both Spanish and English. "Mami," I said, "mi gorda linda." This was the term of endearment I used to call her. The meaning gets lost in the English translation, but it literally means my beautiful fat lady.

She let out a wail.

"I'm going to see you. Te quiero mucho, mami." I said.

She moaned, and it became clear she could not vocalize words.

"Keep talking." The nurse's voice came from the background. "She is responding. She just moved her foot."

Hopeful and holding back my tears, I continued, "Mami, wait for me. I love you, mi gorda linda. The kids love you; we miss you. I am going to see you." She attempted to speak, but audible words were not coming out of her. I continued to express my love for her, trying not to expose the fear that was inching its way into my thoughts. *Is this it? Am I losing mom?* The nurse got on the phone and suggested I make the trip.

After I hung up, I booked the first flight out, which was the following morning. Unfortunately, when I got there it was too late. I missed watching my mama take her final breath by two hours.

Monica's message was that I should get to the hospital as

soon as I landed. The funeral attendants were on their way. I called Monica, "Don't let them take her. I need to see her. Please do what you can to keep her there. I am on my way." I needed to be alone with mom, to hold her hand and give her one last kiss.

At the hospital, the funeral attendants and the nurses were awaiting my arrival. Respectfully, they gave me time and space. Upon entering Mom's room, I dropped my bags and rushed to the bed. There lay my mama, *alone*.

I kissed her cheek and pressed my lips on her forehead, allowing my tears to settle on her face. My love expressed through grief will now forever be with her. Gently caressing her unresponsive hand, I reminisced about a time when Mama was invincible. With my fingers I brushed her lusterless auburn hair, which revealed the gray underneath. I climbed onto the bed and snuggled up as close as I could. Just for that moment, I was a little girl again cuddled up to mom, trying to be still so I wouldn't wake her. I will forever treasure that moment.

While at the hospital, I called my childhood best friend Alicia. She understood the pain of losing a mother. Alicia rearranged her schedule to be with me. In the days that followed, she consoled me and offered advice as needed. Her presence brought me hope—assuring me that my current sorrow would one day become easier to bear.

Monica, a skilled multitasker, stoically handled all the funeral arrangements without letting her own grief show. She knew mom before she became a part of our family. It was mom who brought her and my brother, Diego, together.

While my husband and children were of significant value to me during this season, Monica and Alicia instinctively did what others couldn't. They offered me unwavering support by sharing their life experiences and strengths when I needed it the most. I am grateful for them and how they showed up for me.

PAUSE AND REFLECT
Read Matthew 5:4

1. Are you in a season of fighting a tough battle? Write about what you are going through. If you haven't reached out to anyone for support, who can you call?

2. Write about a time when you knew God placed someone on your path to help you get through a challenging situation.

3. Do you know someone who is struggling right now? In what ways can your life experiences or skills be valuable in helping this person?

I Am Angry, God

Grieving Mom's passing broke the dam that managed my emotions. A sense of numbness and detachment overwhelmed me, followed by periods of weeping. My tears betrayed me and without shame they appeared while grocery shopping, at work, while alone in my car, and interrupted my conversations. Occasional spells of laughter would surface when a memory brought up mom's playful side.

My heart struggled to process what my mind didn't want to accept. Mom was in my dreams and sometimes I stayed in bed longer to extend the dream because we were together, even if it wasn't real. One night, between awake and asleep, I thought I heard her voice in the distance, calling my name. Another time, I felt her presence next to my bed. I wanted to hold on to her. It is difficult to release those we love. Grief breaks us.

I wish mom could have met my grandbabies—her great-grandchildren. I can almost see how she would continuously kiss them and squeeze their chubby thighs. How she would dance out of rhythm to get a giggle out of them and make clicking sounds with her tongue to steal a smile. Oh, the love she would shower them with.

How proud she would be of my children, as she would pursue them with questions about their life, then go back home and brag to everyone about them. I still miss her.

Without warning, anger replaced my grief. It angered me that Mom was in the nursing facility and that she didn't want to stay with me during her recovery.

I was filled with anger towards myself for not putting forth more effort to fight for her care. I grew angry at my siblings because our mama died *alone*.

This wasn't the first time anger took control of the reins in my life. Anger and I have a history together. Many times in my anger, I gave the devil an opportunity to deceive me into wrong thinking and act out in it. I allowed anger to nearly destroy my life during my teenage years and here it was again, conducting my thoughts and emotions in unison.

As I grew older, I learned how to put a lid on my anger and coped by keeping myself busy, such as cleaning the house or going for a run. However, when anger remained bottled for too long, it would erupt into rage. Many times in my rage I would pound the wall with my fists or scream until I couldn't breathe anymore.

We all handle anger differently. Some people resort to food or substances to take the edge off. Some of us shut down, contain our anger, and seal it tight. In certain cases, anger becomes the driving force behind isolation and broken relationships. Anger is one of those emotions we either bottle or blow; we are not sure how to take hold of it.

> Paul writes, "In your anger do not sin": Do not let the sun go down while you are still angry, and do not give the devil a foothold. (Ephesians 4:26-27)

In my anger, I vented to God, doubting His ability to hear or understand me. *There are such evil people in this world, and you took mom! Why didn't you take [ ]...*

I prayed for peace, and yet I felt like my prayers were going nowhere. I continued to cry out to Him even though He felt distant.

I poured and poured my anger before God until there was nothing left. I was empty—anger was nowhere to be found. I had to come to the end of myself, these God-given emotions, to find God waiting there.

If you are in a season of intense emotions, hold on to your faith in God, even when His presence is not felt. God wants you to come to Him. He can handle your anger (rage or any strong emotion you are experiencing). *You have permission to feel angry*. Feeling the emotion itself is not sinful, but our reactions to being overwhelmed by them often are.

PAUSE AND REFLECT
Read Psalms 34:17-19

1. Are you grieving a loss right now? A loss doesn't always mean a death. It could be a dream, relationship, job, children leaving the nest. Journal of this loss and how you feel about it. Don't hold back.

2. What or who are you holding onto that you are reluctant to let God have?

3. Does God feel distant right now? Explain.

4. How do you handle anger?

Before My Beginning

Our lives are an extension of a story that began generations ago. The actions of those in our past affect future generations, whether good or bad. The story of Mephibosheth in the introduction illustrates how the consequences of our ancestors affect our lives. Either way, the good news is that Christ is the end all. The old is gone, the new is here (2 Corinthians 5:17)!

Knowing mom's story helped me to understand her struggles. I have learned to empathize with her challenges despite the negative impact some of her choices had on my early years. The rest of this chapter and throughout this book I will share seasons of her life as she told it to me in bits and pieces, and I have added my perspective.

My mother, an island girl who loved swimming and fishing more than anything, grew up in Cuba. She went to school through fifth grade, yet her limited education didn't mean she wasn't intelligent. Mom had knowledge in the fine arts—which I learned later in life—and had a remarkable ability to learn languages.

At eighteen, she was coerced into marrying William, a Canadian who was twice her age. He had a home in Cuba and got to know mom and her family while on his vacations. Coming from a poor family, my grandmother may have seen this as an opportunity for her daughter to *make a better life for herself* and encouraged this union. Before leaving her island home for Quebec, she gave birth to her first child, Mary.

Mom adapted quickly to life up north. She not only learned English, but became fluent in French. *Pero todo no eran rosas*;

but all was not roses. It didn't take long for mom to realize that her husband was mentally unstable. William's depression kept him glued to the TV for weeks, leaving her to handle everything. Under these difficult circumstances, mom gave birth to her second child, Yvette.

Susan, mom's mother-in-law, made home life even harder by treating her as inferior. Susan easily took control of the home and children as if they were her own. The expectation was that the children be fed, and the house kept clean. William was uninvolved and lacked the mental ability to intervene on mom's behalf. Mom felt stuck, as if she had no other options, and endured the mistreatment.

Over time, as his mental health declined, William had to be institutionalized for treatment. During one of her visits to the psychiatric ward, mom met Lorenzo, a tall, slender, dark-haired man wearing a doctor's white coat. Lorenzo was from Argentina, and was fluent in Spanish. Mom was lonely, homesick, and hungry for her native tongue. A secret romantic relationship developed, and before long, she became pregnant with my brother Alex. Mom initially fell for the deception of this man pretending to be a doctor, when he was really a patient. Despite this, she persisted in the affair.

After Alex was born, mom divorced William, left Quebec with her three children and her lover, and moved to Chicago to be close to family. Most of her siblings had moved from Cuba to Chicago by then.

The relationship with Lorenzo ended abruptly when he committed a crime that resulted in his incarceration.

Months later, mom received a letter from the prison that said he had committed suicide in detention.

Family nearby helped with watching the three young children while she worked as a waitress. Mom was always a hard worker, and life hit her just as hard.

It didn't take long for my birth father, Antonio, to sweep mom off her feet. My father was tall, dark and handsome, very much like Alex's father. Maybe she had a type, and this was it, because before long they were married. And yes, she immediately became pregnant with me. A noticeable pattern (theme) had taken hold of her life. Mom was stuck in a perpetual cycle.

PAUSE AND REFLECT
Read Romans 8:14-16

1. What are some negative themes of past generations in your family? These could be divorce, addiction, suicide, infidelity... Have you noticed these cycles occurring in your life or in the life of your children? How?

2. Are you familiar with your parents' stories? How have their decisions affected your life today—good or bad?

3. God has adopted and restored us through Christ. The sins of our father no longer have a hold on us. Do you base your self-worth on your parents' mistakes, reputation, or on being a child of God? Explain.

A Broken Heart

"Where are my girls?" Mom yelled as she entered the school office. She had been waiting outside for the girls until the last student left the school building. The principal told her that the grandmother had picked them up early. He thought little of it since she was family; the girls acknowledged their grandmother. Susan had slipped into Chicago unannounced and took her grandchildren, my two older half sisters, back to Quebec with her.

Mom spent weeks earning the money necessary to travel and bring her daughters back. The pain was evident in her eyes as she recounted this story to me. "I took a taxi from the airport to their grandmother's house. As we were approaching the house, I saw the girls playing in the front yard. They looked happy to be there." She hesitated, looked away, and then made eye contact with me. I noticed a quiver in her lip that she was fighting through when she said, "How could I take them away?"

At that moment, mom made a split-second decision that forever changed her. She knew she couldn't give her girls the life Susan was providing for them. She didn't have the money or stability. "Take me to the airport." And without stopping to see her daughters or say goodbye, she flew back to Chicago, empty-handed.

All throughout my childhood, she grieved over this decision. On her hardest days, she would gather all the pictures she had of the girls, place them on her bed, and weep. This may have been her way of *spending time* with her daughters.

In her mind, they remained forever young, ten and eight—the age when they were whisked away. It was not unusual for me to find a couple of beer cans on the floor next to her bed in the morning. The beer washed down the sleeping pills she took every night. This was the way mom coped. Mom wasn't the kind of woman who talked about her problems. She kept silent. No one knew of her suffering.

There are things that happen in life that are too difficult to bear alone. No one should suffer in silence. We were created to engage in authentic relationships with one another. Even Jesus, being God, had many friends. Everything Jesus did was an example for us, from cultivating relationships, to loving others, to suffering. Jesus showed us how.

The twelve disciples were his closest friends, the ones he did life with. Within those twelve, Jesus had the three—his *besties*, Peter, James and John. These three men were first hand eye-witnesses and secret-keepers of Jesus' raising Jairus' daughter from the dead (Mark 5:37-43). These were the same three friends Jesus took with him onto a high mountain where He was transfigured before them (Mark 9:2-10). Peter, James, and John had a special insight into the life of Jesus. They were entrusted to keep some matters confidential.

In Matthew 26:37, it says that Jesus "took Peter, and the two sons of Zebedee (James and John) along with him, and he began to be sorrowful and troubled." In this scene, Jesus showed us vulnerability. Jesus opened up to his closest friends and told them how He felt and what He needed. "My soul is overwhelmed with sorrow to the point of death. Stay here and keep watch with me." (v. 38)

Could you remember a time when you shared your innermost feelings and specific needs with a friend?

PAUSE AND REFLECT
Read Matthew 26:36-38

1. What life experience has broken your heart? Who was there to comfort you?

2. Have you had to make a tough decision for someone else's benefit? Write about it.

3. Who are the friends that have insight into your life? Could you be completely vulnerable with these friends without fear of judgment?

Difficult Decisions

Shortly after returning from leaving her girls, mom suspected my father was having an affair. He showed no support or empathy towards mom during her grief and pregnancy with me. Eventually, mom caught them on her bed. This other woman was also pregnant with his child.

In her mental state at the moment, mom wanted nothing to do with him, nor with the baby growing inside her. She didn't want to give birth to me, and went through drastic measures to end the pregnancy. She tried multiple times to abort me, but unlike a previous abortion, it didn't work.

Mom and my father were divorced before I was born. He was completely out of the picture, and never had a presence in my life.

As hard as it has been to process not being wanted, I understand why mom, given her circumstances, didn't want another child. Even though this act had a negative impact on most of my life, I have forgiven her.

I write this story because I know there are others who, like me, have survived an abortion attempt and are struggling through life. Someone who was told they weren't wanted, and who was given details on what was done to keep them from being born. Someone who has felt more dead than alive throughout their life—even after becoming a Christian. Someone who has struggled to find purpose or believe that God really loves them. If this is you, know that there is redemption. You are here today because of Him and for Him: God wants you.

> Isaiah 49:1 says, "Before I was born the LORD called me; from my mother's womb he has spoken my name."

Writing mom's story is important to me because she expressed interest in doing so when I was young. She knew that her redemption story would offer hope to women with similar life experiences—women who were pressured to do something with the promise that it is the best choice; women who found themselves in a desperate situation, made a quick decision, and have struggled with it ever since. If you can resonate, I want you to know there is forgiveness and redemption. You are not alone.

If you are struggling with the aftermath of abortion, there are support groups that can assist with healing. These groups consist of women who have been where you are now, who have healed, and want the same for you. I have met some of these incredible women.

No broken soul is more beautiful than the one that the love of Christ has restored. There is complete healing and redemption in *all things* through Christ.

As an abortion survivor, I respectfully offer my love and support to you. Find comfort and healing for your brokenness in both my story and my mother's. Please listen to these words: You are forgiven.

> Romans 8:1 assures us that, "Therefore, there is now no condemnation for those who are in Christ Jesus, because through Christ Jesus the

law of the Spirit who gives life has set you free from the law of sin and death."

If you are in Christ Jesus, you *have* been set free from the law of sin and death.

You are *not* condemned, and you have access to full forgiveness. This is in the present tense. There is *now* no condemnation. Right now, YOU stand forgiven. Even if you don't believe it, you are still forgiven. Your disbelief doesn't change this truth and what Jesus did for you.

Open your heart to receive this forgiveness and then forgive yourself. Ask God to enable you to do this. If God can forgive you, you can forgive yourself.

If you don't know Jesus this way, remain open to my redemption story, read the Scripture readings, and answer the *Pause and Reflect* questions. I would further challenge you to read a few verses a day from the book of John in the New Testament. As you do this, pray that God would reveal Himself to you personally.

PAUSE AND REFLECT
Read John 3:16-17

1. Write about a time when someone pressured you into doing something that resulted in a negative consequence.

2. Do you believe you are completely forgiven in Christ? If not, read verse 17 again. Why did God send His Son?

3. What is something you can't forgive yourself for?

After Some Time ...

During Sunday morning worship, I closed my eyes, lifted my head toward heaven, and sang praises to my Jesus. It was almost a year after mom's passing, when I experienced a healing in my soul. During this moment of praise I saw mom's beautiful face, smiling the most perfect smile. She looked healthy. The voice within my soul assured me—*She is healed. She is at peace*. Grief fluttered away with that vision.

I walked out of church that morning with a sense of wholeness and a revived heart, knowing mom is at peace. She did not die alone—Jesus was with her, waiting to take her into glory. Intellectually, I knew all this. Just knowing something doesn't always make it feel real or true; it is our experiences that often validate its reality. I had to experience it on a heart level, in my soul, to receive the truth.

God, like a compassionate friend, knew I needed a listening ear—to let it all out. He was listening to my grieving heart all along. *I know, my child. Tell me how you feel. Cry. Scream. I understand. I am listening.* I had to process all that I had been through in my relationship with mom and to grieve her passing in order to be at a place to receive healing.

With the help of the Holy Spirit, I learned to be kind to myself and let go of the guilt I felt for not being more active in her recovery. I forgave myself, knowing I could have done more. Self-condemnation fails to glorify God and diminishes the value of the cross.

If God, through Christ, does not condemn me, why should I continue condemning myself?

The season of losing mom, grieving, and healing created a rebirth in me. It forced me to look at my mortality, and pushed me toward changing the direction of my life.

I want a purposeful and impactful life. I want to fulfill God's plan for me.

The mother who raised me was a different woman than the one who passed away. I saw Jesus' love and forgiveness in her and through her. I am thankful that she chose to surrender her life to Christ, and through this, we will be reunited one day. I'll share more about her transformation in the upcoming chapters, but I want to give you this hope: Mom's situation and her negative cycles didn't last forever. Yours don't have to, either.

> Be strong and take heart, all you who hope in the LORD. (Psalms 31:24)

2

Seeking

I know that my redeemer lives, and that in the end he will stand on the earth. (Job 19:25)

Who Is My Father

"You know, the man raising you is not your *real* father." I was about six years old when my older cousin by two years, Angela, told me, as if she knew I needed to hear those words.

"I don't care." I blurted out.

When I was two years old, mom married Oscar. And as the cycle continued, two children were born into this marriage: Diego and Elena. This was her longest-lasting marriage. They separated multiple times and divorced in my mid teens.

Angela ignored me and continued, "Your real father has a daughter, Sylvia, who is your age." I was relieved to hear this. I had an intuition about Oscar, almost knowing that we weren't related by blood. I couldn't wait to get home so I could ask mom if this was true.

"Mom, who is my real father?" Mom was a closed vault when it came to my biological father. She never mentioned him or any of the other men who fathered her children. It was as if they had never existed. This is one of the faces of shame: pretend it never happened and it will go away. Yet, no matter how tightly we conceal it, the truth always emerges.

Later that week, Alex and I were called into my parents' room. Oscar took the lead as mom sat in silence off to the side. "I am not your real father. I gave you my name. I adopted you." He said, as if he was doing us a favor (*you owe me one, don't forget it*). It didn't feel like an act of love for me, but more like something he had done for mom.

To an outsider, it was obvious we were half-siblings. None of us looked alike, especially Alex and me. We didn't even look like our mother. Having the same last name did not change the perception she was trying to avoid. However, I get it, I understand she was trying to uncomplicate things.

By the time I learned the truth, I already felt resentment towards Oscar. He favored my two youngest siblings, his children, by birth. He showered them with time and affection. They were not given chores or disciplined the way I was. If I said anything in protest about his demands, he threatened to send me away to boarding school.

The news about my *real father* gave me hope. I believed if I could find him, everything would be better. He would protect me. He would love me. I would be complete. My hope was in finding the perfect father. Even if it is false hope, there's something about hope that can get us through difficult situations.

But once Oscar told us we were adopted, there was no information about my birth father. The topic was closed for discussion. He adopted me and the message was that my birth father didn't matter. After that, Angela was my only source of information.

"What do you know about my father?" I asked her when I saw her again. I wanted to know everything.

"Our fathers are brothers, just as our mothers are sisters. This is why we look so much alike." It's true. I resembled her more than my siblings. The evidence for what she said was there in the mirror on the wall.

She lowered her voice to a whisper. "It's like a mystery that my dad is gone also. The story is said that he disappeared around the Bermuda Triangle. I was told he was officially pronounced ... dead."

"So Uncle Miguel isn't your *real* daddy?"

"No," she said. The man raising her was not her biological father, either.

Angela told me my father's full name, Antonio Costas, and that was all I had to go on.

PAUSE AND REFLECT
Read Psalms 27:10

1. Were there secrets within your family? How did they affect you?

2. Was there favoritism shown among your siblings or cousins? By whom, to whom? How did this make you feel?

3. What expectations have you placed on your parents that only God can meet?

The Search

The Yellow Pages was a phone directory that contained the names and addresses of people in a given area. When I realized individuals could be found in this book, I began the relentless hunt for my father. *If he knew where I was, he would come and get me.*

This thick book would show up at our doorstep every year with updated information. In anticipation, I would sneak it into my room and shut the door. I would then flip through the pages, scroll through the alphabet, hoping his name would pop out. I believed this book had the answer I was looking for.

When we traveled, I scanned the hotel room for this book, hoping one day it would reveal to me in big black letters the name I was searching for.

Phone booths were a bonus. They all had phone directories attached to them. Whenever I saw one, like Clark Kent, I waited for the opportune time to slip in hoping I would come out empowered with new information. As if I was making a phone call, I would close the slider door that sometimes caught my hand, and grab the book.

Flip, flip, flip. Glance over my shoulder. Make sure no one is looking. A, B, C, scroll down with my finger. Cossio, Cossman, Cost, Costales... nothing. The names where his was supposed to be were becoming familiar to me. I dreamed of the day I would find his name.

I could just imagine ... *Ring, ring.* "Dad, it's me, your daughter Solé." How happy he would be to hear my voice! "Oh, Solé, I have been looking for you all along, mi hija!" My hope thus fulfilled, it would be my happily ever after.

Gradually, fewer and fewer people even bothered to list their numbers in The Yellow Pages. No matter how hard I searched, the answer remained the same: he was not there.

After years of dead-ends, my hope was re-birthed with the internet. I could extend my search beyond my local town, beyond all the places I might travel.

The old questions resurfaced. *What does he look like? Where is he from? Why isn't he looking for me? Maybe I can find his daughter, my half-sister—Sylvia.*

PAUSE AND REFLECT
Read Romans 15:13

1. What were your childhood hopes and dreams?

2. What did you work hard to get? (grades, parents' attention)

3. Do you believe you need to work hard to get God's attention, or that He loves you unconditionally? How does the way you live reflect your answer?

4. What are some childlike characteristics that you have lost in adulthood? Is trust one of them?

There's Always A Chance

My friend, Annie, who was leading the ladies' Bible study, handed out a white paper in the shape of an egg with these instructions: "Write a prayer you believe will never be answered—a prayer for something you believe is impossible. Then tuck it in your Bible under Psalms 91:4."

> He will cover you with his feathers, and under his wings you will find refuge; his faithfulness will be your shield and rampart.

I didn't have to think hard on this one. *Finding my father.* I wrote it in tiny handwriting, almost embarrassed that this was still an issue for me—*I am a grown woman with a family of my own. I have a heavenly Father. Shouldn't this be enough?*

Through the years, when reading around Psalms 91, I would come across this faded old egg-shaped prayer request, knowing that this would be an impossibility for God to answer.

Over a decade after I penned my prayer, I found a people-search agency online. The website assured me they could find anyone. If they could find anyone, they could find him. Before processing the payment, I closed my eyes and prayed, *God, please let this be it. If I don't find him, give me peace and take the desire of wanting to know who my father is away.* I made a promise to myself that if this agency could not find him, I was done searching.

A few weeks later, I got a lead: The letter I received had the contact information of a person with the same first and last name, although the middle name was different.

In all my years of searching, I had never been this close. Two out of three in the name, I thought, *there's a chance it could be him*. I had an address but no phone number. So I wrote the letter.

Hello, I am looking for Antonio Costas, who was married to Sara. If this is the right person, I would like to speak with you. I am not looking for a relationship, just for some answers ...

I explained who I was, how I found him, and gave him my phone number. My resentment for the way he'd abandoned me coated the words in the letter like sticky paint. If it was him, I didn't want him to feel wanted, but to jar him enough to give me the dignity of a phone call.

I mailed the letter.

New questions, along with the old ones, were filling my mind. *Was this the right person? If not, was I really going to keep my promise to God, or continue the search? Would the person who opened the letter call me, even if it wasn't him? Was I ready to know the truth?* I had a friend whose father passed away right before she got to meet him. Was this going to be my story, also?

With every day that went by, I wondered if today would be the day I was going to get some answers. I was on the lookout for a letter or a phone call. I was on the other end of the search—it was up to him to contact me now. I was waiting for the call I always wished for as a little girl.

This time of waiting allowed for self-reflection. I thought about when this obsession began. I was looking for a father to rescue me. My Savior already did that. I was hungry for the love and security of a father. Daily, I am lavished with love from my heavenly Father. *What was I really looking for?* There was nothing my *real father* could give me that was not already being met by my Heavenly Father. I realized I was no longer in the same place as that broken child from long ago. It was time to let go of the idea of finding my father. I already found him through Jesus.

Sometimes we want something so badly that we miss out on the blessings right in front of us. We often hunger for what we do not have, thinking it is what we need; what will make our life complete. We seek a relationship with someone who mysteriously disappeared from our life. We have a longing to connect with someone that has emotionally abandoned us. We search for purpose and meaning outside of what God gives us.

These pursuits become obsessions—idols that keep us from connecting with the source that offers us answers, and the fulfillment of these longings.

God may be asking you in this season to be still and wait patiently for Him. Maybe there is some maturity that needs to take place before you can enter into what you are seeking. Maybe God has already given you an answer and in your best interest, it is *no*.

In the meantime, God wants us to take delight in Him. He promises He will give us the desires of our heart. The closer we get to Him, our desires begin to line up with His will.

Find peace in God, if He answers your requests, or if not. He is enough.

PAUSE AND REFLECT
Read Psalms 37:3-7

1. What is distracting you from seeing God's daily blessings? (perfectionism, social media, overly committed, negative emotions, a childhood longing)

2. What do you believe is impossible for God?

3. What idols do you need to release from your life? Idols could also be emotions such as unforgiveness and grudges.

4. Do you struggle in the waiting and take matters into your own hands? What does God ask from you?

The Impossible, Possible

"Hello, this is Antonio. I received your letter." Frozen in disbelief, I didn't know what to say. There was excitement in his tone, which surprised me, and I wanted to shout, *"Didn't you know how much I wanted to hear from you?! Why didn't you reach out to me? It's been almost 40 years. Where have you been?"*

He told me how often he wondered about me. He asked about mom. He spoke to me as if we were old friends, as if he had been a part of my past.

Something was not sitting right with me. I sensed a misunderstanding in the way the conversation was going and felt the need to clarify who I was.

"Hold on a minute. Do you know who you're talking to? This is your daughter." I used both names: Choly, the nickname I grew up with, and Solé, because I wasn't sure what name he knew me by.

He paused and everything went silent. He took a deep breath, swallowed, and with a crack in his voice said, "I'll call you back." Then, without giving me the opportunity to say another word, he hung up. I stood there in a state of confusion. *Are you kidding me? After all this time, he hangs up!*

He had been out there all along. *What a dead beat! He was going to disappear again.* I felt hurt and angry. *Why? What was it about me that he was trying to avoid?* I didn't know who he thought I was, but he seemed eager to speak with THAT person. *How could he be that clueless not to realize that I, his daughter, would be looking for him?*

I went from walking in peace by letting this go, to allowing negative emotions from the past to consume me.

The accuser's voice went on the attack: *You were not wanted. You should have never been born.* How quickly we allow our peace to become disrupted! I stood there looking at the phone and breathed out, "God pour your truth into me."

Sometimes we don't get the answers we are looking for. Other times we get answers, but may not be ready to receive what comes. Maybe God and mom were protecting me from him, and I forced this.

He kept his word and called me back later that afternoon. He told me that at first he'd thought I was Mary, my oldest sister. *How could this misunderstanding occur? What would Mary—a girl who wasn't his daughter—want to speak with him about?*

We spoke by phone over the next few months, getting to know one another. I had a memory about a man visiting me at my uncle's house and asked if it was him. It surprised him to hear that I remembered that day.

I did not hold back. I told him about the difficulties during my childhood. It was important to me that he knew how his absence affected me. Yes, my anger was apparent in words laced with sarcasm.

He told me about the time he walked into the bathroom as mom was attempting a self-induced abortion. "What are you doing?" he yelled at her while forcefully pulling her out of the tub. I had mixed feelings about this. He saved my life, only to walk away from being a part of it.

We talked about his battle with cancer and how he was in remission. I asked him about my half-sister, Sylvia.

He told me about her and all his other children. I reached out to Sylvia—she is the daughter of the other woman he had an affair with while married to mom. Sylvia and I became friends.

As the months passed, and my desire to know him quenched, the phone calls became less frequent. It felt best to let things stay the way they were. Ready to move on, I put it behind me for good. We never spoke about meeting each other in person.

PAUSE AND REFLECT
Read Jeremiah 32:26-27

1. Write about God answering an impossible situation in your life. Maybe you received what you needed, not what you prayed for.

2. How does the voice of the accuser rob you of your peace? What does it say?

3. What situations cause you to go into shame? Are there trigger words?

4. Do you believe with all your heart God has your best interest in mind, even when it hurts?

Look At Me

A few years later, I received a call from Sylvia. "Dad's cancer is back and he's in hospice. If you want to see him, this could be your last chance. I booked a hotel room and you are welcome to stay with me." I wanted to see her, and figured this might be the opportunity for all of us to find closure.

I booked the flight to Tucson, Arizona. As soon as I landed I took a taxi to his home. Sylvia was already there and we connected right away. Both of us have a shared interest in health and wellness, as well as a background in finance. I even resemble her more than my siblings growing up. *Without a doubt, we are related.* She told me about hardships she'd gone through while living with him. I thought that even with my difficult upbringing; I had the better end of the deal and felt so much empathy for her.

I met his current wife, an aunt who was delighted to see me, and an uncle. This aunt shared many memories of watching me as a little girl, and I sensed a deep love from her. Even though she knew me, I had no memory of her, yet the way she looked and engaged me acknowledged I was family to her.

As we gathered, Antonio didn't greet me. I couldn't understand why and felt rejected by him *again*. He was alert and engaged in conversations with everyone but me. He gave them all eye contact, but it was as if I wasn't in the room—he didn't see me.

The second day of visiting did not differ from the first. He didn't look towards me, engage in any conversation with me, or acknowledge my presence. He had rejected me my whole life and now he was doing it again.

What was the point of this trip if he was going to ignore me? I became frustrated over this and looked for the opportune time to confront him.

His behavior towards me made no sense. We were not complete strangers, as we had spoken a few years prior. Our conversations didn't end in a negative tone, they just ended. Maybe he never expected to see me in person. For some reason, my presence made him uncomfortable.

At one point, he got off the couch and went into his office. I watched him as he sat on his chair, shuffling through papers on his desk. *This is it!* I got up, entered his office, grabbed a chair, and strategically placed it in front of him. He couldn't leave the room without going past me. He tried to ignore me. With nothing to lose, I spoke my mind.

"The least you can do is look at me," I told him. I placed my hands on his cheeks and guided his face toward my face. What a strange experience this was for me, as I am sure it was for him. There was no mistaking the resemblance between my father and me. I wasn't sure what I was feeling at that moment, but I remember thinking, *this man's blood runs through my veins, yet I don't know him.* A part of me grieved for something I didn't have and would never have from an earthly father.

As our eyes connected, he wept. I held his gaze, allowing my tears to flow with his. Once he regained his composure, he said, "How can I look at you? I am so ashamed of not being there for you. I let you down. Can you please forgive me?" In shame, he turned his face away and reached for a drawer with cash in it. "Here, let me give you money for your trip."

I placed my hands firmly on his cheeks again and redirected

his face back towards mine. Our eyes locked. "I am not here to condemn you, but to set you free."

I didn't know where those words came from; it was an inspired moment, a divine intervention. After I said those words, a heaviness was lifted from him and I saw his face transform from distressed to at peace. Then he wept again, perhaps with tears of relief.

Somehow, I can't help but think he needed me there to forgive him more than I needed to meet him.

PAUSE AND REFLECT
Read Philippians 2:3-4

1. How can God use you as part of someone's redemption story?

2. Reflect on a time when you received grace or felt undeserving?

3. How do you speak truth in love?

4. Have you ever done a good deed intending to bless someone and received the greater blessing? Write about it.

After Some Time ...

Coming from a large Cuban family, my memories are of Cuban coffee, pig roasts, salsa dancing, lots of cousins, and family gatherings for any and every occasion. We always greet each other and say goodbye with a kiss. Cubans are loud, which expresses our passionate nature. Along with our boisterous, noisy chatting, we communicate with over-the-top hand gestures. I definitely picked up this mannerism!

During my childhood, I spent a lot of time at my aunt and uncle's house on my mother's side. My cousins were my closest friends. I remember a particular day at my uncle Pedro's house that always stood out to me. I was in the living room and the adults were whispering in the kitchen with a man I had never seen before.

Something was wrong: Cubans don't whisper. Being the intuitive child that I was, I felt a sense of secrecy—something important was happening. There was urgency in the air. I wondered if someone died and they were trying to figure out how to tell me.

My aunt Elena introduced me to him. "Choly, this is a friend of ours."

"Hi, Choly, how are you doing?"

"I am fine."

"I am moving far away and stopped by to say goodbye to your Uncle Pedro and Aunt Elena. May I sing you a song before I leave?"

He sang me an old Spanish song called *Cielito Lindo*. I gave him my undivided attention. In my young mind, I wondered if he was a famous singer. Why else would a stranger want to sing me a song? I remember him caressing my face—not in a creepy sort of way, but heartfelt. I was too young to understand, but I never forgot this visit from the man who sang *Cielito Lindo* to me. I have one childhood memory of the mystery man who turned out to be my biological father.

Today, I have a perfect Father. He chose and adopted me to be His daughter. I am called by His name and am the apple of his eye. He forgives and loves me unconditionally. My hope is in Him. He will never leave me nor forsake me. He is my strength and my healing. I have unexplainable peace in the One who created me and to whom I belong. He has redeemed my life, and I am complete in Him. He is my *real* Father.

The answer I was seeking didn't come from a book called The Yellow Pages, it came from the book with words in red—the Holy Bible. Your Heavenly Father and life's answers can be found in this book.

I want you to know your Heavenly Father is easy to find. Whether He will be available or not isn't a mystery, and you don't have to second guess if He will abandon you. He didn't create you to figure out life alone but to be in an intimate relationship with Him.

I can testify to the truth of this verse, and you can make it your own, too:

> A father to the fatherless, a defender of widows,
> is God in his holy dwelling. (Psalms 68:5)

3

Identity

Do not fear, for I have redeemed you; I have summoned you by name; you are mine. (Isaiah 43:1)

What's In A Name

"Hi. I'm Solé. Nice to meet you."

"What?"

"Solé," I repeat, a little s-l-o-w-e-r and LOUDER!

"Sally? I'm Jennifer."

"Not Sally, Solé. S-O-L-E. With an accent. So-lay. Solé." I often have to repeat my name over and over and spell it before people get it.

"Solly? Oh, that's different. What does it mean?" This is a common question I get when meeting someone for the first time.

Once in a while I meet someone who knows someone or has heard of someone with my name. It has become more common today. However, I also get, "That's such a beautiful name."

"Um-hum," I used to say with a forced smile, avoiding eye

contact. I didn't always welcome this compliment.

Through the years, I have fabricated the intended meaning of my name. "It means sun. In Spanish *sol*, French *soleil*, and *sole* in Italian."

I lay it on thick, so the conversation doesn't go any further. "So my name means sunshine." I would reply with a passive annoyance of *let's get past the introductions*.

I can't share the true story behind my name in thirty seconds and I don't always want to. So I fake it; smile and say what people want to hear. Don't judge me. We all do this. How often do you tell people you are fine when you are not?

My birth name is Solé, the shortened version of Soledad. In Spanish, this means solitude, alone, or loneliness. The name I was given, Solé, came from pain, not celebration.

To my surprise, there is someone in scripture with whom I can relate with when it comes to names: Jabez. When I first discovered his story, I read it multiple times. *Yes, all two verses*. Something resounded within me and it was more than just his name.

God communicates with us through His word. He often brings you to the same scripture verses because He is speaking to you through it. As you read your Bible, ask the Holy Spirit to illuminate what He wants to show you.

We can find the story of Jabez in the tribe's genealogy of Judah in 1 Chronicles 4:9-10.

> Jabez was more honorable than his brothers. His mother named him Jabez, saying, "I gave birth to him in pain." Jabez cried out to the God of Israel, "Oh, that you would bless me and enlarge

my territory! Let your hand be with me, and keep me from harm so that I will be free from pain." And God granted his request.

Scripture tells us she "gave birth to him in pain." Childbirth is painful. While I would agree that some births are more painful than others, and this could very well be the case with Mama Jabez, somehow I can't help but see something different in this prayer.

What if Mama Jabez had a different kind of pain? Like most of us, she was a woman who likely had a difficult life. Could she have been dealing with an unplanned pregnancy because of rape? Maybe she lost her husband, and she was facing parenting alone. What if she didn't have the resources to care for another child? We only know she was in pain when she gave birth.

Jabez means pain or sorrow. In Hebrew, sorrow can also mean grief.[1] So Mama Jabez was grieving something; she was in sorrow. Grief and sorrow are emotional pains, unlike the physical pain of labor, which she experienced in birthing her son.

The last part of Jabez's prayer caused me to wonder about this plea. "Keep me from harm so that I will be free from pain." *What pain were you asking God to shield you from, Jabez? The birthing pains your mother had?*

I know, and Jabez knew, he would never experience this kind of pain. So what pain is he asking God to keep him free from?

Jabez' prayer was that if God can keep him from harm, he will also be free from pain. Yes, I could repeat the same prayer today! *Lord, keep me from harm so that I may be free from pain.*

All that harms us, pains us. Did Mama Jabez tell him she was in pain because something harmed her? Was Jabez the result of this harm?

I wonder if his name, Jabez, was a reminder of an adversity his mama experienced, and his name, like mine, was the storyline he was born into. My perception from reading his prayer is that Jabez felt the emotional pain or trauma his mama went through so much that it caused him to cry out to God. When we cry out to God, He hears!

And ... God granted his request. Now we don't know if God answered at Jabez' first cry, but we do know that this was an *after some time* moment of redemption. I just love this! God knew the sorrow Jabez lived with, heard his prayer, blessed and redeemed his life. All this in two Bible verses. Just imagine all God wants to show you in the 31,102 verses of the Bible.[2] Don't let this number overwhelm you—two verses can change your life just as it did for me.

My name was connected to mom's hardships from before I was born. I experienced my mother's pain because of it—her emotional suffering. The pain, fear, or trauma we carry can be passed down to the next generation.

PAUSE AND REFLECT
Read Psalms 139:13-18

1. What is the story behind your name? Does it bring you joy or shame?

2. Write about areas of your life where you are just going through the motions, *faking it*.

3. God created your inmost being; He knit you together and knows every part of you more than you know yourself. He created you for a specific purpose. How does knowing this change the way you see yourself?

It's Just A Name

Throughout life, we take on many names. Names can give us a sense of power or can weaken us. They can make us feel loved or strip away our self-worth. We can be *sister, daughter, aunt, wife, mother,* and *Mimi* (what my grandchildren call me).

Our profession assigns us a title, which is just another name that we sometimes use to identify ourselves. *Doctor, Coach, Teacher, Nurse, Author,* and *Speaker.*

A bully may issue us a name that sticks: *Teacher's Pet, Nerd, or Slut.* Some of us get nicknames in an effort to point out a flaw: *Bucky Beaver, Four Eyes.* Names given to children, whether based on physical features, mental aptitude or in just plain teasing, remain difficult to erase from their memory.

In school or by a doctor, we are labeled as *lazy, stupid, dyslexic,* or with *Attention-Deficit/Hyperactivity Disorder.* These names can limit our potential when we use them to identify ourselves.

What about the names that bring joy? Don't you love to be called smart, sweetheart, my love, beautiful? If you've been called these names—those that revive you—I bet you are smiling now. Your heart overflows with joy just thinking about them. These names speak life into us.

In elementary school, Alex and his friends used to make fun of my nose by calling me Pinocchio. With a tough-girl attitude, I would say, "Sticks and stones may break my bones, but words will never harm me." Even though this was a short-lived sibling teasing, it hurt. The negative names we are called cause more damage than sticks and stones thrown at us ever will.

I recently came across a thought-provoking poem that Brendan Byrne wrote and Lauren Child used in the Ruby Redfort series.

This poem expresses the pain of name calling.

> "Sticks and stones may
> break my bones, but
> words can also hurt me.
> Stones and sticks break
> only skin, while words are
> ghosts that haunt me.
> Slant and curved the
> word-swords fall, it pierces
> and sticks inside me.
> Bats and bricks may ache
> through bones, but words
> can mortify me.
> Pain from words has left
> its' scar, on mind and
> heart that's tender.
> Cuts and bruises have not
> healed, it's words that I
> remember."[3]

Reading this poem evoked feelings I had not felt in a long time. Words haunt, they pierce, they stick in us, they mortify, and ultimately scar us. Hurtful words linger in our memories.

PAUSE AND REFLECT
Read Isaiah 49:1

1. What are some names/titles you go by?

2. What are some hurtful names you were called as a child? How have these names affected the way you see yourself? What dreams have they kept you from pursuing?

3. What are some positive names/statements people have called you?

4. What name does your inner child long to hear?

Charlie

"What have you done to my daughter?" mom yelled at my stepfather, Oscar, as she grabbed me to get a closer look. "Her hair will grow out thicker," he explained. I was about three years old when Oscar shaved all my hair off. As I got older, mom made it a point that I knew how much this bothered her. "I was very upset that he shaved your hair. We got into a big fight over it." He did not have permission to alter my looks in this way, making my hair even shorter than my older brother.

This buzz cut made me look like the hairless cartoon character Charlie Brown. Alex gave me the nickname Charlie. In his broken English, it sounded like Choly. The name stuck like a brand, and I was called Choly by my family, extended family, and friends. Only in school was I called Solé.

This nickname was more damaging than anyone could have imagined. It was not only the name itself, but what it represented. *I looked like a boy*. In addition to that, I was sometimes dressed in boy's clothing. They could have been Alex's hand-me-downs. I don't know. Nevertheless, it was a confusing impression of myself and had a negative impact on my self-image.

As a young girl, I naturally gravitated towards dolls, dresses and all things *girly*. I loved to make crafts, color vibrant beautiful pictures, play house, dance—often in a leotard or tutu—and sing. I loved wearing bright outfits; flower patterns were a bonus. Even when wearing the most dainty dress, when I looked in the mirror, I didn't see a pretty girl. I never did. I saw the shaved-head image from when I was young. As I got older, what I saw in the mirror never changed. I didn't see my feminine features.

> Trauma can cause us to see ourselves as flawed; to see an image that does not fully represent what is really there or who we really are.

In my thirties, I had an unexpected *after some time* redemptive breakthrough with this part of my story. Upon entering my bedroom, I saw my daughter Hannah looking through my childhood photo album.

With no thought of what was sliding out of my mouth, I said, "Didn't I look like a boy?" As she was ready to flip the page, a picture grabbed my attention. I placed my hand on it to let her know I was still looking at it. There before me was a little girl with an inch of new hair growth. *Innocent*. I saw when the twinkle in her eyes faded. When her beauty was stolen. I saw what broke her heart. I saw all that her young life had already experienced. I saw her.

For a minute, it was just her and me. Compassion for that little girl from the past welled up in my soul. Seeing those pictures through a different lens—seeing the truth—allowed me to pour love into my inner child.

We all have an inner child that longs for love and acceptance or even validation. This inner child needs to hear the truth of who she is. She needs to hear it from you.

As my daughter noticed my deep reflection over the picture, she asked, "What's wrong, mom?" I would answer this question for her one day; just not then. At the time I said,

"Nothing, I'm fine."

As she continued turning the pages, I was in a whirlwind of thoughts. Images of different stages of growth were projecting in my mind: as a little girl, when entering puberty and my body began showing outward signs of my femininity, and into womanhood. That picture showed me when I first believed the lie—when the trauma happened. I was holding on to a distorted image of myself because of what someone did to me, and the name I was called afterward. This negative thought pattern blinded me from seeing and loving myself properly. Up to that point, I saw myself through the lens of brokenness. *I am damaged goods*. I didn't feel worthy of being loved and believed that God made a mistake when He created me.

Later that evening, alone in my room, I walked towards my dresser mirror. With my hands on the dresser, I stood in front of the mirror and looked into the eyes of the woman staring back at me. For the first time in my life I saw beauty, strength, and tenderness flowing out of me. I saw redemption! My features didn't change at that moment. My heart did. I saw the truth of who I am, of how God made me. I never looked like a boy to my Father! He saw the little girl He created. He saw the woman I had become and finally, so did I.

Healing and reconciliation from my past to the present took place at that very moment. I had a new awareness of how this negative thought pattern emerged, developed, and ultimately took me captive. I wondered what other areas of my life had been captive to the lies from the past.

Most people are bound by lies that grab a hold of them through words or events. These lies attack our identity and derail us from God's purpose. They contradict God's truth.

Paul tells us to "take captive every thought to make it obedient to Christ." Prior to writing this, he reminds us that the war we are waging is in the spiritual realm:

> "For though we live in the world, we do not wage war as the world does. The weapons we fight with are not the weapons of the world. On the contrary, they have divine power to demolish strongholds. We demolish arguments and every pretension that sets itself up against the knowledge of God, and we take captive every thought to make it obedient to Christ." (2 Corinthians 10:3-5)

Whatever lie you are believing about yourself is a stronghold in your life. Right now, stop feeding it and wage war! Demolish this stronghold that is setting itself up against the knowledge of God—what He says about and who you are. Seek this knowledge in the Bible. Pray that God would reveal to you through the Holy Spirit the truth of who you are created to be.

PAUSE AND REFLECT
Read Ephesians 2:10

1. What is a name you identify with?

2. Do those around you see you as this name? What do you think they see?

3. Do you perceive yourself in a negative light because of what was done to you? How do you see yourself?

4. You are God's masterpiece. There is no name given to you that changes who God created you to be. It is up to you to trade in the lies for the truth. What are some lies that are holding you captive? What does God say about them?

La Loquita

The waves began rocking the boat from side to side. In fear of it tipping over, I quickly stood in the center of the boat with my legs spread out and arms extended to steady it as I cried in terror. "La loquita!" my step-father said. "Look at her," and laughed. His words prompted my siblings to laugh at my fear.

Oscar labeled me as the crazy one, *la loquita*. He would call me this any time I showed emotion. I was called crazy for being scared during horror films, for crying when he hurt mom, for trying to break up their fights, for expressing myself through creativity such as dancing, for getting upset over all the chores he was giving me ... Over time, the rest of my family followed along. They didn't know. They were doing what he did.

I am an empath. An empath is a person who feels a higher level of empathy for others. Empaths pick up on people's energy, both positive and negative. We have a strong sense of discernment, intuition, and care from deep within.[4] I used to think having these strong, out-of-control feelings was a curse. *Something is wrong with me.* No one in my home understood it. I didn't either, or know what to do with them. Mom told me I loved *too* much. I was *too* sensitive. Oscar used my empathy for others against me, and any time it surfaced, it just gave him another reason to call me *crazy*. It was as if he was trying to convince everyone, including myself, that I was crazy.

Over the years, I wore out. I struggled with depression from a young age, not knowing how to deal with *all that was happening* and everything I was feeling.

I wondered if they were right. I questioned my sanity, and

those questions kept me silent.

"Go clean the boys' room," Oscar would command. Sometimes I was compliant, other times I was angry and resentful.

"Leave her alone, she does enough," Mom would say to tell him to back off.

"She will be a wife one day and needs to learn how to do these things," Oscar would often say, giving me another chore. To keep the peace, mom let it go. We never knew what would set him off. I did what I was told in order to protect my mother.

He did whatever he could to break me emotionally. "You weren't wanted. Your mother tried to abort you." I heard it first from him, even before I understood what abortion was. But I understood what it meant when he said "you weren't wanted." This made me feel as if I was alone.

The things that were said caused the most pain—the attack on my identity. Unfortunately, I followed suit and became my own abuser by giving myself names that continued to harm me. Names like ugly, uneducated, worthless, and, yes, crazy.

In our brokenness, we unknowingly do what is done to us. We *act out* and fall into the negative cycle of abusing ourselves and/or others. We grow critical, resentful, and withdraw. We believe and feed lies that blind us from the truth. This is just where the enemy wants us.

I want you to know that if you believe something that goes against what God says about you; you are believing a lie! All lies come from the enemy—he is a liar and the father of lies (John 8:44).

The enemy will attack your identity first because you are created in the image of God, ultimately this is an attack against

God.

The lies we face are our *Goliath*, and all it takes is one rock, Jesus Christ, to knock them down. Children of God, let's crush these lies!

PAUSE AND REFLECT
Read Isaiah 64:8

1. What themes have you noticed in your life?

2. What names pull you into a negative cycle?

3. You are uniquely designed by God. There is and never will be anyone like you. Your life has purpose and matters. Do you believe this?

Re-Named

What we have done, however horrible our sin may be, does not define us. Our worth is not determined by what others have done to us or what is said about us. It doesn't matter if we were born into poverty or wealth, money does not define us, either.

A disability or disease does not define us. Our profession (even if we are a brain surgeon) does not define us. Whether we are single or married, have children or are a pet mom, these are not our defining qualities. In heaven, these *earthly things* are dim, in the light of eternity. Our identity—what defines us—is eternal and comes only from who we are in Christ.

> Therefore, if anyone is in Christ, the new creation has come: The old has gone, the new is here! All this is from God, who reconciled us to himself through Christ and gave us the ministry of reconciliation: that God was reconciling the world to himself in Christ, not counting people's sins against them. And he has committed to us the message of reconciliation. We are therefore Christ's ambassadors, as though God were making his appeal through us. We implore you on Christ's behalf: Be reconciled to God. God made Him who had no sin to be sin for us, so that in Him we might become the righteousness of God. (2 Corinthians 5:17-21)

Because of Christ, we are reconciled to God. There is nothing that can get in the way from the reconciliation that comes from God. There is no debt outstanding on our behalf; Christ paid for our sins in full. Therefore, our sins are not counted against us. A clean slate every day! Bye-bye, old life. Later, labels. No more negative names. The new is here!

We are Christ's ambassadors. Wow, what an honor! Even though there is nothing I can do to make Him love me more, this title given to me makes me want to represent my Father with integrity. It makes me want to live for Him and give Him the glory for everything in my life.

The Merriam-Webster meaning of ambassador is:

1. *:an official envoy*
   especially: a diplomatic agent of the highest rank accredited to a foreign government or sovereign as the resident representative of his or her own government or sovereign or appointed for a special and often temporary diplomatic assignment

2. *a: an authorized representative or messenger*[5]

We are given immediate position and purpose. We represent Christ. Our message is Christ. It is all about Him and for Him. And in this, we become God's righteousness. Yes! Reading this puts a smile on my face and releases any heaviness I am carrying.

Along with being a new creation and Christ's ambassador, here are some "I am" statements that I identify with:

I am saved and secure. I am a child of God. I am chosen. I am the light of the world. I am free from condemnation.

I am clothed in righteousness. I am transformed. I am forgiven. I am loved. I am victorious. I am more than a conqueror. And my favorite is, I am redeemed!

I am all these things and so are you! This is who God says we are. These statements encourage my heart when I am struggling. I hope they encourage you as well. I pray that as you continue to dig into the Scriptures, the Holy Spirit shows you *your* identity in Christ, and that you ground yourself in life giving names.

PAUSE AND REFLECT
Read 2 Corinthians 5:17-21

1. Sort through all the names thrown at you and replace them with the truth of who God says you are. Even if you don't agree or believe it, it doesn't change how He feels about you or who you are in Christ.

2. Names are important, they have meaning. There are many names by which God calls Himself. What are your favorite names for God?

3. Write some of your favorite "I am in Christ" statements and claim them.

After Some Time ...

Today when someone asks about my name, I say it means *Son shine*. They hear sunshine and that is fine by me. When I think about my name, I see Jesus, the Son, shining His light over me—a light illuminating my path; a light exposing lies from my life; a light that darkness flees from. This is my redemptive name.

If a name has caused you pain, reframe it!

I no longer allow my childhood nickname, what my step-father used to call me, or any of the demeaning names I have called myself to control me. Even though they make their appearances now and then, I know where to find the truth to demolish these lies. I no longer carry the shame my name used to hold. Those names no longer haunt, pierce, or mortify me. Yes, there is a scar, but *redemption* is written all over it.

Names matter even God calls Himself by many names. These names describe His attributes, His divine nature, and His character.

Here are some of my favorite names of God:

> *El Roi* - The God Who Sees Me (Genesis 16:13)
> *El Emunah* - The Faithful God (Deuteronomy 7:9)

> *Jehovah Goelekh* - The Lord Your Redeemer (Isaiah 60:16)
> *Jehovah Sali* - The Lord My Rock (Psalms 18:2)
> *Jehovah Uzzi* - The Lord My Strength (Psalms 28:7)
> *Jehovah Jireh* - The Lord Will Provide (Genesis 22:14)
> The Alpha and Omega/The Almighty (Revelation 1:8)[6]

Here are some of my favorite names that refer to Jesus:

> The Word (John 1:1)
> The Bread of Life (John 6:35)
> The Good Shepherd (John 10:11)
> The Light of the World (John 8:12)
> The Son of God (Matthew 3:17)
> Savior, Messiah, The Lord (Luke 2:11)

Here are some titles for the Holy Spirit:

> Advocate, the Spirit of Truth (John 15:26)
> Spirit of Wisdom and Revelation (Ephesians 1:17)

The gifts God has blessed us with also describe us. I have the gift of empathy. I am an empathetic woman. It is not a curse.

It is normal to feel what others are feeling; to sit with them in their pain. Healthy empathy allows me to connect with others while not allowing their pain to overwhelm me. I have learned to help people carry their burdens, not do all the carrying. Thank God for your gifts and bless others with them.

Don't skip this chapter without taking to heart what God calls you and without embracing your identity in Christ. Through prayer, ask God to reveal to you the special names He has for you.

4

Secrets

Praise the LORD, my soul, and forget not all his benefits—who forgives all your sins and heals all your diseases, who redeems your life from the pit and crowns you with love and compassion, who satisfies your desires with good things so that your youth is renewed like the eagle's. (Psalms 103:2-5)

If People Knew

OH, THE POWER OF secrets. Every time Oscar said, "Don't forget how I found you," mom retreated. She was under the spell of that threat—that he would expose her secrets to everyone so that people would see who *she really was*. This threat paralyzed her from speaking her mind. She became a prisoner, not only to Oscar, but to the secrets of her past.

Oscar had something on her that empowered him, and he used this to oppress her. He knew how to keep mom in this shameful, secret-keeping cycle in order to have his way and continue to abuse her. I saw how this damaged her.

I never knew what it was, and didn't think it was appropriate to ask her. If she wanted me to know, she would have told me. Then again, maybe she did. Anyway, we shouldn't share everything with just anybody, yet hiding everything is dangerous to our inner being.

We keep secrets to avoid from being exposed. We back off, cower, and disguise our true self, thinking, *if people knew ...*

Those three words hold us captive. We give our past permission to control us. We believe the lie that the secrets we're keeping will protect us or someone we love. We put a lock over our lips in order to keep our secrets under control, but then the secrets shackle us. We are no longer keeping them—they are keeping us.

I know firsthand the damage of being kept by secrets. Secrets are not like emotions that we can bottle up. Once *bottled*, emotions ferment intoxicating us from the inside out: anger becomes rage; sadness becomes depression.

A secret is an incident or circumstance that we keep hidden because of the shame it can bring upon us or others. Like mold, hidden things sprout and grow, causing damage.

> What if we saw secrets as a story that should be told in confidentiality with a safe person; a person who has the best interest in mind of the secret keeper?

Besides allowing people to control us, like Oscar did with mom, secret keeping can breed destructive behavior. My destructive behavior began with self-harm, then during my teenage years progressed to drug and alcohol use, which led to promiscuity. The emotions that followed these actions were disillusionment, hostility, inferiority, disgust, depression, and dullness.

When the kept secrets wanted a voice, cutting gave me some

relief. The toxins had to come out. When I spiraled into depression because of the things I could tell no one, drugs and alcohol diluted the poison brewing inside of me. One negative action had to outdo the other in order to appease the original secrets and then the ones that followed. This was the lethal cycle the secrets kept me in. Cutting, drugs, and alcohol became their own secrets, establishing even deeper cycles. I was stuck in a destructive pattern of self-condemnation.

Let's look at John 3:17 once again:

> "For God did not send his son into the world to condemn the world, but to save the world through Him."

This is worth repeating: if you are in Christ, your secrets do not condemn you. The beauty of the gospel is that all sins, even the *if people knew* sins, are forgiven and redeemed. We have a new life—He has made us new. We are no longer bound by our past, our sins and secrets. God is not keeping a record of our wrongs; He has reconciled us to Himself. The inability to accept this truth will continue the negative cycle in our life and keep us captive to our *if people knew* secrets.

PAUSE AND REFLECT
Read Romans 3:23-24

1. Are you keeping *if people knew* secrets, or are they keeping you? Write them down. Consider this exercise as a toxin purging.

2. What methods do you use to keep secrets under your control?

3. Does anyone use your past to shame you or keep you under their control? Could this person be you?

4. In your need to be heard, have you shared a secret with the wrong person? How did you feel afterwards? I have done this many times and have learned to be selective when sharing. Please use caution in "giving dogs what is sacred and throwing your pearls to pigs" (Matthew 7:6).

5. How does knowing that "all have sinned and fall short of the glory of God" help ease your burdens?

Domestic Violence

"Stop it! Stop fighting!" I would yell, running in between them, and extending my arms to create a separation. "Don't hit my mother!" I wanted the fighting to stop.

The bruises or stitches didn't keep mom from her responsibilities. Some mornings, I would sit on the toilet seat and watch her get ready for work. Mom would simultaneously rummage through her make-up bag and inspect her face in the mirror. Her hand automatically went for the Cover Girl foundation which was a few shades darker than her pale ivory skin tone. Generously pouring the liquid into her hands, she would spread it over her face and neck, as an artist does to change the color of the canvas. Mom outlined her tired eyes with thick black eyeliner and wore heavy mascara, hoping to deter from her swollen eyelids. She preferred beet red lipstick, which also served as a blush. She would highlight her cheekbones with the lipstick and then smooth it out evenly with her fingertips. Even then, the bruises would bleed through the foundation, making parts of her face look darker than the rest.

> Domestic violence affects more people than we realize. Physical, sexual, and verbal abuse, including coercion to do things that are harmful to you, your children, or someone else, all fall within the lines of domestic violence. It's not limited to your partner and can come from any family member or person you live with. Both men and women can become victims of an abuser.

Domestic violence exists in all neighborhoods, regardless of affluence or poverty. The abuser often keeps the victim under a close watch and isolates them from family and friends. Even when the abuser apologizes, cries, and says they will change, it often escalates. This is the pattern of an abuser; they promise to change in order to keep the relationship and continue the abuse.

Perhaps someone you work with is living this nightmare. Maybe it is happening within your family circle or you may be living in terror, hoping it won't happen again but knowing that it will. If you are in this situation and have a trusted friend, reach out to them.

This is not an *if people knew* situation, this is a *you need to get out now* circumstance in which you need to bring the abuse into the light of day as soon as possible; right now, today. Even if you're not sure how you will get to work or the kids will get to school. Your safety must come first. Your abuser can promise all they want—that they'll change. They will continue to say those things, but you *must get away*. Yes, an abuser can reform, but they don't need to struggle through that redemption process on your time. If you stay, you're telling them that the change they promise isn't really necessary if they want to keep you. What is being inflicted on you is not your fault, and you do not deserve this. You don't need your abuser; you need to be safe.

It wasn't as easy for a woman to leave an abusive relationship when I was growing up. Women's support groups have grown across the United States and worldwide in the last few decades.

There are organizations that help women find safe housing and guide them in becoming self-reliant. You can find some of these in the resources section at the back of this book. You can also find local support groups in your area by doing an internet search or through your local church.

If you are in this situation, chances are there is someone waiting to help you. A friend of mine shared how she got out of an abusive marriage only after she confided in a family member. That person suspected something all along. People are more aware of abuse these days.

Sometimes we think we are covering it up, but those closest to us know better. It wasn't until my friend realized she had to do something and be willing to take the risk that those who loved her came to her aid. In situations like these, we cannot receive the help we need unless we ask for it.

Her family members set up a safe place for her until they could secure a place in another state. She had to testify in court regarding all the abuse she and her children endured. She did it with an army of support behind her.

Her support system empowered her to leave, take legal action, regain control, face her abuser, heal, and live again. This can be done for you. Help is available, and you do not have to do it alone.

If any of the above applies to you, please don't think, *my situation isn't that bad*. Don't let pride or shame stop you from seeking help. Chances are those around you know or suspect that you are struggling. They may be waiting for the green light to enter your situation and help. They know that until you ask for it, an offer of help won't be worth much. They need to know you want out, and they know that you have to be the one to say it.

"I want out. I'm done. No more. This is not okay. I will not wait for my abuser to change any longer."

I wanted mom to leave Oscar, and I spent many years resenting her for not doing so sooner. Over time, the resentment fermented into hate.

When I was in my early teens, mom divorced Oscar. He was out of the house for good. However, it didn't keep him from coming around now and then. He still held some power over our lives.

PAUSE AND REFLECT
Read Philippians 4:19

1. What have you been covering up lately?

2. Are you in an abusive relationship, or do you suspect that someone you know is? If so, what is one thing you can do to make a change?

3. Do you believe your situation is unique and you cannot possibly share it with others? Do your excuses sound like these: *What would people think? Or He/she is really not a bad person, he/she just has bad days.*

You Too?

Over coffee, my friend Heather blurted, "I could have killed him." By the tone of her voice and the shifted expression on her face, I knew—no, let me say—I *felt* what she was saying. We both became silent, filtering our emotions from anger to rage, then dipping into compassion for one another and the wounded little girl in us. There was a connection we shared. We didn't have to say anything. We *understood* each other. We welcomed the silence that was needed at that moment, a silence that normally might have felt awkward.

Weeks before this experience, I arrived at the gym early to prepare for a class when I noticed Lisa waiting for me. Lisa, an accomplished business owner, looking as sharp as always in her stylish clothes and flawless make-up wanted to talk.

We had time to chat, and the conversation went deep fast. It was as if she had one chance to say the words, otherwise they would forever stay locked inside. "If I had a gun, I would have pulled the trigger." That was not what I would have expected from this beautiful, over-achieving professional.

What we present on the outside is not always an accurate reflection of what is going on inside. Women know how to fake it. As my mom would say, "I don't have time to go crazy. I have to keep it together to put food on the table." While inside, she was losing her mind! We pretend, we stuff, we cover our pain with make-up, nice clothes and a successful career to mask and push down our pain—our secrets. We feel alone, ashamed, and empty as we battle a war within ourselves. *If people knew* ... we struggle in silence.

Lisa's words gave me permission to share that I, too, have wanted to pull the trigger. At sixteen, I wanted to wipe out my childhood abuser. Her experience was with an abusive ex-husband. They had been divorced for over a decade, yet the painful memories, *the poison*, was oozing out. Lisa's story reminded me of my friend Esther, who also had an abusive husband, and over tears one day told me that her life would be better if he were dead.

These are four stories from those of us who went to that terrifying place in our thoughts, but I know that there are many others. I often felt I was alone with the part of my story that I wanted a person *gone*. Even though I had a different situation from these women, I understand those feelings—to be consumed by hate; to be driven by anger; to be kept by secrets. I had been in that place for many years and wondered, *What kind of human was I to have these thoughts.*

These ladies' honesty validated my anger from a time in my life God has since redeemed. And in return, my story validated theirs. We all share parts of each other in our story. There are threads that connect us to one another. We share similarities, whether we are talking about trauma, parenting, relationships, or hobbies; we make connections. The only way we can know that we are not alone is by sharing our story. This is God's design for us—to have meaningful relationships, to live in community with others. This is where healing begins.

PAUSE AND REFLECT
Read Matthew 7:1-5

1. We socialize with those who have similar interests to ours. Have you unexpectedly connected with someone that was a complete opposite to you? What were your connections?

2. Do you have a close friend that you misjudged when you first met? Explain. First impressions are just that, impressions. We really don't know someone until they take their mask off.

3. Share about a time someone misjudged you. How did it make you feel?

4. Ask God to reveal to you where you tend to judge others, and why? Does it stem from jealousy, anger, or conflict with that person; or do you struggle with self-righteousness?

Life Is Tough

I know life is tough. If you haven't experienced tough times—just wait, they will come. In the meantime, don't judge others who have done things you would *never do*. Without experiencing what they have, you can't determine your own capabilities.

> Extend compassion to those who are struggling; rally around them and offer the support you would want in that situation.

Sometimes, in our innocence, we enter a difficult situation, like mom did at eighteen. We get pressured into something with the promise of a better life. Not wanting to disappoint, we keep up the façade that everything is fine. We believe the lie that *we are trapped* and *this is just the way it is*, instead of knowing that our circumstances can change—we can change them.

Tough times can come by our own making. We give in to a variety of pressures, such as sexual promiscuity, because we are hungry for approval and connection. Out of a sense of despair, sometimes we make it worse for ourselves, even knowingly doing things that will have negative consequences. Instead of admitting our mistakes, we repeat these harmful patterns and continue the destructive cycle.

Most of the time tough times just come. We are born into a difficult situation. We become the target of someone's anger or the victim of someone's perversion.

The reality is, we have suffered undeservedly. These are the consequences of living in a fallen world.

Although I wouldn't wish hard times on my worst enemy, I can attest to God's faithfulness in this—we don't have to face our struggles alone. Through Jesus, the current path we are on can merge with God's grace, forgiveness, healing and purpose for our life.

> 1 Peter 5:10 says, "And the God of all grace, who called you to his eternal glory in Christ, after you have suffered a little while, will himself restore you and make you strong, firm and steadfast."

After we have suffered, He will restore us—redemption! He will make us out-of-the-fire, under pressure kind of strong, like a diamond! This is when we shine best, *after we have suffered a little while*.

Yes, seasons of suffering can strengthen us and draw us closer to God. I have grown from every hardship, even though it wasn't easy and I couldn't see the positive in every struggle. My personal experiences have led me to believe that redemption happens *after some time*. Our sufferings serve a greater purpose as it brings us closer to God, helps us grow, and inspire hope in others.

PAUSE AND REFLECT
Read 1 John 1:8-10

1. What tough times have you experienced because of someone's choices?

2. What tough times have your choices brought upon you?

3. What tough times has life given you?

4. Which of your most difficult life experiences brought you closest to God?

A New Foundation

Mom never stopped searching for the truth. The truth finds us when we need it the most. It is how we respond to it when it shows up that matters.

Shortly after mom divorced Oscar, she became a sold-out believer of Jesus Christ. Her faith empowered her to break free from anyone else's control. She discovered the difference between religion and a relationship with God through Jesus. Religion pointed her to a punishing God. Relationship with a loving Savior is what she needed, and this is what she lived the rest of her life.

Mom shared her new faith boldly and became involved in the church. Eventually, she started church planting in the community. Local pastors respected her efforts in sharing the love of Christ.

One time, when visiting me, she asked if I had an extra Bible. "What did you do with yours?" I asked her.

"I gave it to the lady next to me on the plane. She never heard of Jesus and I introduced her to Him."

Yep, that's my mom.

The beautiful thing about mom's faith is that she loved unconditionally. This was something I struggled with as I watched her live it out. I didn't understand it yet. She easily forgave those who hurt her and gave without expecting to receive. She fed her enemies—literally. Love and grace became her message.

Mom was like the woman who wept at Jesus' feet. She was forgiven much, therefore she loved much. We find the woman's story in Luke 7:37-47.

> A woman in that town who lived a sinful life learned that Jesus was eating at the Pharisee's house, so she came there with an alabaster jar of perfume. As she stood behind him at his feet weeping, she began to wet his feet with her tears. Then she wiped them with her hair, kissed them and poured perfume on them. When the Pharisee who had invited him saw this, he said to himself, "If this man were a prophet, he would know who is touching him and what kind of woman she is—that she is a sinner."

There it is: "Jesus, *if you only knew* ..." The finger-pointing, shame-slamming Pharisee was mumbling under his breath. Ladies, the enemy has been using this line for a long time. But the woman who was weeping knew something powerful: she knew that Jesus already knows. From creation, God knew your situation. Stop letting the enemy shame you and give God your burdens. You are forgiven and are loved. Jesus already *knows*, and His love for you remains unchanged. Period.

Jesus knew what that judgmental Pharisee was thinking, then He told them a parable about a moneylender who canceled the debts of two men. Neither of them could pay him back. One owed him five hundred denarii, and the other owed fifty.

Here's the kicker: "Now which of them will love him more?" (v. 42).

It's not a trick question, though perhaps Simon thought it might be. Simon replied, "I suppose the one who had the bigger debt forgiven" (v. 43). YES!!!

> Then he (Jesus) turned toward the woman and said to Simon, "Do you see this woman? I came into your house. You did not give me any water for my feet, but she wet my feet with her tears and wiped them with her hair. You did not give me a kiss, but this woman, from the time I entered, has not stopped kissing my feet. You did not put oil on my head, but she has poured perfume on my feet. Therefore, I tell you, her many sins have been forgiven—as her great love has shown. But whoever has been forgiven little loves little" (vv. 44-47).

Mom got it. Once she understood this kind of forgiveness, she received it and offered it to her offenders. Mom began building her life on a solid foundation.

PAUSE AND REFLECT
Read Luke 7:36-50

1. Are you practicing a religion, or are you in a relationship with Jesus? Explain the difference.

2. Could you relate more with the Pharisee or with the woman at Jesus' feet? Explain your answer.

3. Do you still have the same passion you did when you first came to know Jesus? What has changed?

4. How can your *if people knew* secrets be used to encourage someone?

After Some Time ...

I am forever grateful that mom allowed God to break the chains that kept her bound. She was finally free—free from shame, free from secrets, free from domestic violence. Her life was a picture of God's redemptive power.

With God's help, mom did the hard stuff—she removed herself from a threatening situation. Her secrets became her testimony. God gave her the strength and perseverance to provide for her family. She pursued her children and did the best within her power to restore broken relationships.

Her decision affected my life, the lives of my children, grandchildren, and our future generations. When I see my granddaughter praying to Jesus it reminds me of the promise that, "He (God) is the faithful God, keeping his covenant of love to a thousand generations of those who love him and keep his commandments" (Deuteronomy 7:9).

After some time also means that there's something better for a future generation, perhaps a baby who isn't even born yet or a child who will do great things. It could be for a wounded teenager that desperately needs a Savior or for a broken woman who is at the end of her rope and Jesus is extending his hand. This is why Jesus came to earth—to set us free.

Allow God to set you free from shame and those secret things that have kept you in bondage. Do the hard stuff and go to him. He is waiting for you.

And ... when the devil or anyone else whispers *if people knew* in your ear, you say out LOUD, "Yes, if people knew what Jesus has done! If people knew what Jesus can do! If people knew what happens *after some time* of walking with Jesus!" People *need* to know.

5

Hard Times

In your unfailing love you will lead the people you have redeemed. (Exodus 15:13)

I Want Out!

> Why did I not perish at birth, and die as I came from the womb? (Job 3:11)

I HEAR YOU, JOB! Your cries resonate with me.

I know the pain and agony that cause you to question your own existence and believe death is the only way out. Like Job, I have pleaded with God to relieve me from my anguish. Yet I have never walked in his shoes; my journey has given me this sorrow. For most of my life, I responded with an *I want out* mindset. Thankfully, God put people in my path at just the right time to keep me here.

While writing this book, two women have shared with me their, I want out, stories. Becky, who is in women's ministry, asked to meet for coffee. Temptation got the best of her and she fell into an affair that she didn't want to let go of. In her shame, the only resolution was to end it all. My other friend, Helen, an accountant who had all the material possessions you can imagine. The Better Homes and Garden house, new cars, a beautiful family, a thriving career; yet something was missing. These *things* were not meeting her inner longings and checking out seemed like the best solution. Thankfully, these ladies didn't follow through. Jesus met them right where they were. Through the power of the Holy Spirit and Christian counsel, they got to the root cause of their distress. Becky broke off the affair and reconciled her marriage, and Helen established deeper roots into her faith, which has given her life real meaning.

Listening to these women and reading Jobs' account confirms that people struggle with suicide ideations. It is also a relief to know that I can be raw and honest with God, just as Job was. I can allow myself to process my feelings regardless of how angry, despondent, or ungrateful I sound. He hears. He cares.

When we open up and talk about our struggles, those around us may take a chance and talk about theirs. Just as I am sharing my past struggles in this book and Becky and Helen shared with me, you can share yours with a friend. Your vulnerability in sharing your pain invites them to do the same. We need each other to heal and overcome, and sometimes we need the help of a professional.

During a dark time in my young adult life, I didn't trust myself to be alone. I told my husband to put the guns away and scheduled an appointment to speak with a counselor.

To this day, I cannot remember her name, yet she was like an angel that showed up at just the right time. What I remember is when she said, "When the body is sick, we seek treatment, we figure out the problem and care for it. When our mind is sick, we ignore it. We keep it to ourselves. We need to care for the mind as we do for the body."

It didn't take long to see that I was caught in a *perfect storm*. The triggering of an undealt past event combined with coming down with the flu set everything in motion. When emotionally triggered, running often allowed me to process my thoughts and provided stress relief. Because of being sick, I hadn't exercised in over two weeks. To make matters worse, I was premenstrual. I was a sick, emotional, hormonal mess, and my feelings of checking out made perfect sense to me. This could be the case for any of us. A slight imbalance can tip the scale, overwhelming us into believing that checking out is the best option.

The counselor suggested that I have two people to turn to when I'm feeling hopeless. My husband was my number one person, and I called a friend to be my number two. This is a friend that I could call at any hour of the night and she would run to my side. No shame, no questions, no judgment, only love and support. We need this support system on hand because we get triggered, sick, stressed out, and have hormonal imbalances that can bring out the crazy in us.

Chances are you or someone you know is struggling silently or engaging in self-destructive behavior. There is no shame in this. We have fallen into a trap believing that if we are dealing with mental illness; we are less Christlike. There has been this stigma over Christians and mental health that just allows the enemy to grab a foothold over our lives. I have met people that would agree their life is great and still have suicidal thoughts.

Listen, we all struggle with our thoughts and mental health. If you haven't yet, be thankful! If you cannot understand mental illness, it doesn't mean it is not real. Whatever your position is on this topic, extend grace to those who are in the trenches, not only because we are called to lift each other up, but because one day you may need this kind of grace.

If you are at your lowest point, please hang on and speak with someone. Seek the help of a professional. I want you to know that, whatever your situation is, it can get better. Jesus made it clear, in John 16:33, "In this world you will have trouble."

Trouble will look different for everyone. We cannot avoid it. No one is exempt. The rest of John 16:33 continues with an offer of hope. "But take heart! I (Jesus) have overcome the world."

Through Jesus, we can overcome the troubles of the world. Hope is waiting, even when we cannot see it. It may not be today, tomorrow or next year, it may not be the answer we are seeking, but, *after some time*, you will overcome!

PAUSE AND REFLECT
Read Job 3 and 2 Corinthians 1:3-4

1. What situation has caused you to want out?

2. Do you struggle with depression, anxiety, suicide ideations or anything of this nature? If so, have you shared these struggles with anyone? If not, when will you do it? Make a plan today.

3. What are your thoughts or experiences on seeking professional help? Do you believe a professional can guide you towards healing?

4. Job lamented over his sufferings. Write or share with a friend about a time when you were at the end of your rope. This may be hard to share, but remember, your story is an offering of hope for someone else. Not only that, someone who may resonate with you can offer you hope.

Tears That Save

"Auxilio! Auxilio!" Help, help! Mom yelled as she ran from Oscar's fists. Her cries for help and the yelling between them echoed in my head constantly. Mom's screams would wake me up at night. There were times I would hear them fighting, even when it wasn't happening.

I was about seven years old when I ran outside to get away from the commotion. On the back patio of our house, there was a half wall that I climbed with the help of a chair. From the half wall, I pulled myself onto the roof fixing my eyes on the power lines. I thought, *If I could touch them, the noise in my head—the fighting—would be gone.*

On the roof, I inched my way towards the edge. Alex, who was also outside, heard me crying, and instantly looked up at me.

"What are you doing?" he asked as I reached for the web of wires connected to the roof.

"I want to die. I can't take this anymore." I stretched my fingers in an effort to make them long enough to grab the black cable.

"Please come down." He fell to his knees as tears rolled down his cheeks. "I beg you to please come down." He cried, clasping his hands together and pressing them towards his chest.

Seeing his tears prompted me to get off the roof. His tears were a sign of his love for me. His crying and pleading saved my life, and I am thankful for him.

It wasn't by chance he was there. I don't believe things happen by chance. We may never know the impact we can have on another person by being in the present moment with them.

> One of the most profound ways to provide comfort for someone is to show your love through tears.

When my husband, Duane, was going through uncertain health issues, my friend Linda wept with me. Her tears expressed her love for us. They told me, *"I will be with you through this and help carry your pain."*
Just as Jesus wept with Mary and Martha, tears show someone you empathize with them. It lets them know you hurt with them. Tears express love. Tears convey what words cannot.

> Jesus wept. (John 11:35)

I feel this. I feel the love and compassion He had for Lazarus and his sisters. Jesus loves us in the same way.

PAUSE AND REFLECT
Read John 11:33-36

1. As you reflect on your life, who encouraged you to keep moving forward?

2. Do you have a hard time crying in front of others? Why?

3. Write about a time someone shed tears for you, with you? How did it make you feel?

4. What do you imagine it looks like when Jesus weeps for you?

Just Hold On

From sixth grade on, the predator called depression was a constrictor wound tightly around my body, suffocating the life out of me. I could not see past my pain—the future never existed in my mind. I was living in a state of hopelessness. Mom didn't see the signs. The bed wetting, withdrawing from the family, and the self-inflicted cuts on my arms and legs.

I met Alicia the summer going into seventh grade. Besides my cousin Angela, Alicia was the first friend I had up to that point in my life. We became inseparable. Our circle of friends thought we were sisters, and we went along with it.

Her father regarded me as a daughter. He suspected abuse and left an open door, allowing me to stay at his home for days on end, which I did. Whatever he did for his daughter, he did for me. He bought me clothes for back-to-school, gave me movie money, and treated me to meals with the family. Anything I needed, he didn't hesitate to provide for me. He recognized my value as a human, and I grew to love him as a father.

Alicia's wisdom and encouragement kept me going. She was the only one that knew about my struggles. "Just hold on. I promise life will get better." She would assure me when I wanted out. She was offering me a hope I knew nothing about. I tried holding on to these words. I trusted her.

If you are struggling, reaching out to a trusted friend is a good starting point. However, if your friend assumes your mental health issues are due to sin in your life, kindly find another friend to speak with.

Right or wrong, this accusation, this judgmental response is not what you need at the moment; it only heaps more shame upon you just when shame is not what you need. If she tells you, "You need more Jesus, and then you will be better," thank her for the advice and walk away. While I agree that we all need more Jesus and sin can enable mental decline, these responses will not aid in getting to the root cause of your situation. Healing is a process, and this legalistic approach often overlooks the deeper issues. There are people that Jesus uses to help us overcome our darkest days. They are out there. Don't give up seeking help!

God placed Alicia and her father in my life. Their home was a safe haven, a place where I could sleep peacefully. The constrictor didn't squeeze as hard in this home, which allowed me to catch my breath—if only for a short time.

PAUSE AND REFLECT
Read Matthew 25:35-40

1. Who was there for you during your teenage years?

2. What wisdom did you receive as a teenager that you still refer to?

3. Do you believe Christians who struggle with mental illness have unresolved sin in their life? What do you base this belief on?

4. Journal about a time you were "one of the least of these" and someone offered you hope.

5. *Just hold on*, were the words that kept me going. Jesus held on for you and me. We will never understand that kind of mental, emotional, and physical suffering. Do you ever look at the cross amid your own suffering?

I'm Done

"Choly, wake up. Did you take these pills?" Holding an empty pill bottle, mom nudged my arm to get me to respond to her.

"I am tired. Let me sleep." I slurred.

Just hours before mom arrived home from work, I grabbed a bottle of pills out of the medicine cabinet. *Shake, Shake, Shake.* I could hear that it was full. I opened the bottle and poured half the pills into my hand. Using my other hand, I arranged the pills on the cabinet shelf in piles of five, one on top of the other. I did the same with the second half. When the bottle was empty, I threw it away. While looking at myself in the mirror, I swallowed each pile with water, until there were no pills left.

Mom didn't leave my side that evening—I felt her presence nearby, and she had been praying for me the whole time. The following morning, I woke up feeling weak and sick to my stomach. I threw up a few times and stayed in bed for a few days. It was the depression that kept me confined to my bed.

I had dropped out of high school, was struggling with substance abuse, and isolated myself at home. Scripture tells us to "be alert and of sober mind. Your enemy the devil prowls around like a roaring lion looking for someone to devour" (1 Peter. 5:8). I was not alert or sober-minded, and the enemy of my soul was devouring me. *You have nothing to live for. You have nothing to offer. You are all alone.*

In Luke 4, there are key verses in resisting the enemy. The devil tempted Jesus during His forty days in the wilderness, looking for His weakest points. This is still his strategy today. If the enemy is daring enough to tempt God, don't think you are exempt. Be alert! And do not isolate yourself—this makes you easy prey for a prowling lion.

This first thing we must do is to be filled with the Holy Spirit. Jesus confronted the devil "full of the Holy Spirit" (v. 1). Initially, we receive the gift of the Holy Spirit upon repentance and acknowledging Jesus Christ for the forgiveness of sins (Acts 2:38). We fill ourselves daily by reading the Bible, through prayer, and being connected to the Spirit all the time. The Holy Spirit is our helper, advocate, and source of power (Acts 1:8). In order to ward off the enemy and grow spiritually, we need to be *plugged* in to this power.

Next, we need to know our identity in Christ and how to handle doubts. The devil tempted Jesus with food and questioned His divinity. "If you are the Son of God, tell this stone to become bread" (v. 3). When we are feeding our soul through prayer, scripture reading, and fasting, the enemy dangles a carrot to entice us away from God. How many random thoughts enter your mind when you are pursuing God? Yet, when working on a project or at your job, you have full focus, *no carrots*. These distractions take our eyes off the One who gives us spiritual nourishment and whose we belong to. We feed our soul and find truth in God's word.

In the second temptation, the devil tempted Jesus with the allure of worldly status if He would "worship him" (vv. 6-7). Oh yes, status, success, riches ... we are all guilty of wanting these—of wanting more. This is an easy temptation for most of us. After all, we live in this world, we have to be a part of it, right? God makes it clear, "Do not conform to the pattern of this world, but be transformed by the renewing of your mind. Then you will be able to test and approve what God's will is—his good, pleasing, and perfect will" (Romans 12:2). We renew our mind by, you guessed it, reading the Bible, and it is there where we discover that we are to worship only God (v. 8). This implies that we are not on the throne, or anyone else for that matter.

The last temptation was about power and questioning God. The devil tried to cast doubt about whether God would show up and show His mighty power, "throw yourself down from here" (v. 9). It is easy to doubt because we have not seen God. It is much more difficult to live a life of faith.

> "And without faith it is impossible to please God, because anyone who comes to him must believe that he exists and that he rewards those who earnestly seek him" (Hebrews 11:6).

Don't test God to prove He exists. Have unwavering faith in Him, and you will reap His rewards.

God becomes visible through spiritual eyes as we delve into the Scriptures. The point I am emphasizing is to make reading your Bible and memorizing scripture a daily habit. Jesus set the example for us as He threw scripture back at the devil.

"It is written: 'Man shall not live on bread alone'" (v. 4).

"It is written: 'Worship the Lord your God and serve Him only'" (v. 8).

"It is said; 'Do not put the Lord your God to the test'" (v. 12).

When the devil had finished all this tempting, he left him

until an opportune time (v. 13).

He came back for Jesus and will come back for us. The good news is that the devil is defeated and with the help of the Holy Spirit and Scripture, we can resist him.

PAUSE AND REFLECT
Read Luke 4:1-13

1. Does substance abuse play a role in your life? Are you ready to work through it? Who can you talk to about getting the help you need? (There are resources at the back of this book.)

2. What keeps you in bed? What are the things you avoid because they seem too overwhelming?

3. When overwhelmed, what is the enemy whispering in your ear? What scripture verses can you memorize to counter these tactics?

4. Do you actively read the Bible and memorize scripture? Why is this important?

5. What are things you get *filled* with instead of the Holy Spirit?

Tears That Heal

"I am sorry for all that you went through." I didn't realize those were the words I longed to hear from mom. This was the first time I felt an authentic connection with her. She cried for me, with me, and wept over my childhood.

Every summer, while my kids were growing up, mom would visit for about two weeks. In our own brokenness, it was common for us to argue during her stay. We both held onto unresolved anger and resentment from wounds that were never discussed. This unseen tension between us was a reminder of our own brokenness.

During one of our disputes, I fired a handful of darts. "You were not there to protect me." *Bullseye*. "You didn't give me the love I needed." *Bullseye*. "How could you not see what Oscar did?" *Bullseye*. "You tried to abort me." *Bullseye*. Even though my aim was flawless, I did not feel like a winner. I wanted to take those words back, but the damage had been done. I pierced her heart and I felt the pain. Startled by what she heard, mom walked to the edge of my bed and sat down. Silence.

I realized the little girl in me was crying out.

"Mama, can't you see me? Tell me you love me."

Through tears, I apologized and allowed my inner child to speak.

Mom listened with profound empathy. I saw it in her eyes. In the past, when I tried to address these issues (though never being this aggressive), her response was, "You don't know what a hard life is." She was probably right. While her life may have been more difficult, it shouldn't devalue my wounds. We cannot put a gauge on someone's pain. If you have been hurt, no one can tell you that your pain is insignificant.

During our conversation, I felt as if I had permission to take a peek at her life and began asking her questions. "Mom, tell me. I want to know about your hardships." I wanted to understand her, and at that moment a conversation arose between us in complete vulnerability.

She told me about her first marriage, the affair, my father, her first abortion, the abortion attempts on my life, and the challenges of living with my step-father. She told me things I would never write about. This was the only time we spoke about these things. We were at peace with what took place that day.

I hugged her, and through tears, entered her pain. "I am so sorry you had to go through all that." I finally understood her. I cried for her and with her over her hard life. Love and forgiveness for each other patched the broken pieces of our relationship, leaving the past behind us.

God redeemed my relationship with mom in an unexpected way. God knows our hearts and what we need even before we have words to express it.

> He fulfills the desires of those who fear him; he hears their cry and saves them. (Psalms 145:19)

PAUSE AND REFLECT
James 3:2-12

1. Do you throw darts out of pain, to manipulate or intentionally hurt others?

2. Is there someone that comes to mind from whom you need to ask forgiveness for hurtful words said?

3. What is the little girl in you crying out?

4. Is there a relationship you would like to see redeemed?

After Some Time ...

As I reflect on my life, I can see that there has always been a destructive pattern. This pattern was set in motion in my mother's womb as she was convinced that aborting me would be the best decision for her. Then, in my early years, due to home life dysfunction, I believed taking my life was the only way to get relief. Finally, because of unresolved childhood trauma, depression took hold of me during my teenage years. This became a stronghold, something I couldn't seem to shake off.

Scripture tells us that the thief (enemy) comes to kill, steal, and destroy (John 10:10). The enemy will bring up what he can to defeat you when you are alone, tired, and emotionally drained. He aims to distract you from the truth when you're at your weakest. The good news is that John 10:10 doesn't end with the enemy.

> "I (Jesus) have come that they may have life, and have it to the full."

Jesus promises life and to the full! Hold on tightly to the promises of God. These promises have kept depression away. It's been decades since I have felt despondent.

Years ago, I made a vow to never utter the words, "I want to die" again. I set a personal boundary that I would speak words that give life, not tear it down. The first time I caught myself reverting to the old pattern of thinking, I stopped and expressed gratitude for my life. Then I said out loud, "I am thankful for my life. God has given my life meaning and value. I love myself. I am loved by God and others. I want to live!"

This was a powerful, life-changing exercise. When I said it, I felt it. This statement became real for me and I have proclaimed it over my life.

Death will come one day—no need to rush it. Until then, I will live to the glory and honor of the One who breathed in me the breath of life.

I want to challenge you to create your own life-giving statement and read it out loud. Write it on a note card, read it often, and place it somewhere visible, such as the bathroom mirror, refrigerator or front door. Have this statement as the screensaver on your phone.

Since making that promise to myself, I wake up every morning filled with gratitude for my life, and the possibilities it holds, even on challenging days.

Psalms 118:17 is a take-action verse for those of us who have struggled with suicide ideation:

> "I will not die but live, and will proclaim what the Lord has done."

If we were to sit down and write all that the Lord has done, we would see His actions throughout our lives. These are the proclamations of hope we offer to those who are reaching for the power line: In Jesus, we have access to a different power—the Holy Spirit! Not a power line that will stop your heart, but a power that will start your heart beating in a new way.

Write your life-giving statement. Then post it where it will inspire you every day.

6

Religion or Relationship

In him we have redemption through his blood, the forgiveness of sins, in accordance with the riches of God's grace that he lavished on us. (Ephesians 1:7-8)

Getting Out Of The Heat

"Why are all these people here?" I asked Angela during one of our childhood outings.

"Not sure. Let's get in line and find out."

I followed her lead.

This neighborhood cathedral, with its stained-glass windows and hand-carved doors, provided a cool escape from the South Florida heat. The double doors were always open, inviting us to come in.

This church had become a pit stop during our bike riding escapades. The coolness of the building brought much needed shade from the scorching summer sun. The silver bowl at the entrance, encased in wood, contained life and energy for us. A splash of the water on our parched skin revived us, extending our adventures for the day.

This morning was different. The typically vacant church

had people seated in the pews and others standing in line down the center aisle.

I stood behind my cousin and followed her every move. When she took a few steps forward, I took a few steps. While waiting, I stepped out of the line to see what the people in the front were doing. I noticed every person had a chance to speak with the priest—or that is what it seemed like from where I was standing. When it was Angela's turn, I couldn't hear what he said to her, but she nodded her head yes, as the person in front of her had done, then she opened her mouth and he put a wafer in it. She turned around and walked toward the entrance of the church. When it was my turn, I didn't understand what the priest said. Just as Angela and everyone before me had done, I nodded my head yes, opened my mouth, and allowed him to put a wafer in it. The wafer attached itself to the roof of my mouth like a suction cup. Prying it loose with my tongue, I walked towards Angela, who was waiting for me by the front doors. We mounted our bikes and were off to another adventure.

Our family was not religious. Mom would occasionally say the Lord's prayer at bedtime with us. She would recite a verse and have us kids repeat it until we said it all the way through. I had no idea this prayer was in the Bible.

There was no depth to this prayer. No explanation to what it meant. No testimony, history, or roots to understand it. *Who is this father we pray to?* I know she believed there was a God, but she didn't know him as a loving Father. "God will punish you," she said, when I misbehaved. "God will punish you if you don't obey me," she added, to make me behave.

God was a punitive God in her eyes, and it became this way

for me—a distant, angry God waiting to punish me every time I did wrong. This did not attract me to knowing Him, so I was not interested in *religion*.

This church was close to the house we called "La Finca," the farmhouse. It was a two-bedroom house surrounded by groves of mango, lime, lemon, and banana trees. La Finca is one of my earliest memories. My baby sister, Elena, was born when we lived there and my aunts, uncles, and grandmother lived nearby.

Oscar had some violent episodes at this house. His rages would get out of control. One Christmas, he demolished a ping-pong table, which was a gift to the family. He jumped on it until it collapsed and continued breaking it to pieces with his hands. He once pushed my grandmother as she tried to protect her daughter. This was the last time she interfered on my mother's behalf. His tantrums filled me with fear.

During one of their fights, to escape the turmoil at home, mom ran to the church. She returned with the man dressed in black with a white collar. I found it odd seeing this man in our home. The only thing I knew about priests coming over your house was from what I had seen on TV—where they performed exorcisms. So, as a young child, I believed Oscar was demon-possessed and the priest came over for an exorcism. I didn't stick around for what was about to happen! It seemed to work for a little while, but the demon came back. Even so, I learned you can run to the church for help.

PAUSE AND REFLECT
Read Romans 1:20 and John 1:1-5

1. When you look at the world around you, what convincing evidence stands out to you regarding God's role in the creation process?

2. What are some of your early memories of the church?

3. Are your beliefs about God influenced by personal experiences or teachings?

4. Do you see God as a punishing God, waiting for you to mess up?

Prepare The Soil

"Do you want to go to Bible School?" Angela asked a few years after our bike riding adventures. I had spent the night at her house and she told me about the school bus coming to pick up the neighborhood kids. "We sing songs, do crafts, have a snack, and listen to a Bible story."

"Sure, why not?" *Did I have a choice, being at her house and all?*

When I got on the bus, the children were charged up and in the middle of a song. Synchronized hand motions added to the energy. I felt as if I fell into an episode of the Twilight Zone. I didn't know the songs or hand motions, so all I could do was stare. And stare I did. *What kind of religion is this?*

I was well aware of many spiritual schools of thought. Mom dabbled in many religions, not committing to any of them. She was always seeking. Mom would take me to seances which were held in dark rooms where women could speak in men's voices. These places reeked of cigar smoke, which would stick to my clothes. Mom also had her spiritual-enlightenment yoga practice and every once in a while we would hear about another religion. Mom was open to anything that might offer the answers she was looking for. This often led her further from the truth.

Angela's mom was a santera—a high priestess of the Afro-Cuban religion of *Santeria*, which was most familiar to me growing up. Santeria involves rituals of percussion music alongside trance-like dancing, casting spells, animal sacrifices, and food (especially sweets) offered to the "saints."

What has Angela gotten me into now? I thought, knowing we were too far from home at this point to get off the bus. The joy and energy of the children and adults on the bus made me feel uncomfortable. Not that I didn't experience joy in my life. I did. But this kind of community, in particular, was very foreign to me.

It felt like the bus ride took forever. With each stop, more children were added to the harmonious frenzy that I was trying to understand. Finally, we arrived at the local high school gym where Bible school took place.

In the gym, there was a set of tables against the wall with craft materials on it; another set of tables on the opposite side had water pitchers, cups and snacks; and carpet squares were laid out for story time in the center.

During craft time I laced together a leather coin purse which had a daisy imprinted on it. I don't remember what the snack was, but I will never forget the Bible teaching based on Matthew 7:1.

"Do not judge, or you too will be judged." *Did God know I was judging them already? Is God going to punish me?* This verse stuck with me.

Hebrews 4:12 tells us that "the word of God is alive and active." I heard the living Word that day.

By the end of the day, I was glad I went to Bible School and was hoping I could go back. I wanted to learn the songs, the hand motions, and know more about what they were teaching. Mom picked me up, and I had to go home that evening. It didn't occur to me to ask permission to spend the night again so that I could go back to Bible School the next day. I never went back.

Throughout our lives we may encounter Bible verses before we understand what they mean.

Most of us have seen John 3:16 displayed on TV during live recordings of football games, TV news shows, or other events where an audience is present and able to share this good news by simply writing it down on a poster board.

This is one way God pursues us—through others and the living word.

PAUSE AND REFLECT
Read Hebrews 4:12

1. Did you ever hear or know scripture before realizing it was in the Bible? What was it?

2. What are the first Scripture verses you learned? What is the surrounding memory?

3. Write about a time when God's word spoke to you in a specific situation.

4. What is your favorite Bible verse? Why?

Plant The Seed

"Yes, you can stay with us. I will pick you up at the airport." When I was about ten years old, mom reconnected with *the girls*. I remember how eager my siblings and I were to finally meet our older sisters, Mary and Yvette. I couldn't even imagine the thoughts or emotions mom was processing through knowing that she was days from seeing her girls. Until then, I had never spoken to or seen recent pictures of them.

When the day came, I went to the airport with mom to pick them up.

"Look, mom," I said, pointing towards two young women in the middle of the crowded airport. "That's them."

"It can't be," she said as we walked in that direction.

"Yes, we are looking for two women, and there they are." *Was mom still looking for her little girls?* They made eye contact with us, recognized their mother, and began walking in our direction.

I stood there watching as they hugged one another. *How does it feel seeing your mother after ten years? How does mom feel seeing her little girls, now women?* I tried to process the emotions of the reunion and my role in this event. I was excited about meeting them, but didn't really know who these women were. After all that time, mom didn't know them either. However, today I know this was an *after some time* moment of redemption for mom and the girls.

The one thing that brought us all together that day was blood relation. In a similar way, we believers are brought together by the blood of Jesus. We don't know each other and may never meet on this side of heaven, but this doesn't change our relationship to one another. We are family.

The girls were *Christians*. I didn't know exactly what a Christian was. I thought it was just something you either were or weren't. They were good, and we were bad. They were Christians, and we were not. I thought only good people had access to God and the Christian life.

This became something my siblings and I made fun of behind their backs. They were proper, well-mannered, no cuss, no fuss. We were wild kids. Undisciplined. Ruthless. Some of us cussed more than others, and sometimes we misbehaved just to get a reaction from them. We quickly learned what pushed their buttons. For example, Diego would share with them the tasteless jokes he often heard from mom. Even if I didn't think they were funny or appropriate, I laughed along with him.

They continued to visit us throughout the years—we didn't scare them away. Yvette even lived with us for a time while attending a local university.

On one visit, Yvette gave me a small book entitled *Soul Food*. I didn't know it was the New Testament. This book didn't look spiritual; the cover featured a picture of people smiling, with apartment buildings in the background. I read some of it and found some stories more interesting than others. I must have lost this book in one of our many moves. Even so, another seed had been planted without me even being aware of it.

PAUSE AND REFLECT
Read Mark 4:3-20

1. Have you ever experienced persecution because of your beliefs?

2. What family members are on the outside looking in? Do they see that you are good or do they see Jesus?

3. In The Parable of the Sower, what seed does your life reflect most? The one that fell on the path, rocky places, thorns, or good soil? Explain.

Thorns And Thistles

Many years went by with no thoughts of Bible School or *Soul Food*. I filled the void inside me with whatever drug I had access to.

Once mom divorced, I had no further contact with Oscar. The only time he came around was to pick up his children, Diego and Elena.

Diego and Elena developed a habit of giving their father food from our refrigerator when he came around. This angered me. Mom worked two jobs to sustain us, and I worked to help mom with the bills. Oscar had no right to the food we were buying, but it didn't seem to bother mom when I told her about it. This infuriated me.

Did she forget how he used to beat her? How awful this man had been to her? And what about me? But she didn't know about *that*.

I had seen the movie *The Burning Bed*[1], the true story about a battered wife named Francine Hughes. Her ex-husband had come back into her life after an accident left him unable to care for himself. Since he was the father of her children, she allowed him to stay with her, but as he recovered from his injuries, the abuse started up again. At her breaking point, she told the kids to go to the car and wait for her. She then set fire to the house while her ex-husband slept in her bed. At the murder trial, she was acquitted based on temporary insanity. Parts of that movie hit close to home, and I felt for Francine Hughes and her children.

In my depravity, I fantasized about poisoning my step-father's food the next time I had the opportunity. I didn't want that man coming around. *What if mom decided to take him back?* Perhaps I did have some sort of temporary insanity going on!

Unresolved trauma thwarts our ability to see clearly. We see only the injustice, the offense, the offender moving on with life; yet we want justice served, we want *vengeance*. Our minds become fixated on what payback would look like. We continue to re-victimize ourselves by dwelling on conversations or events that occurred. We rehearse what we should have said or will say the next time we have the chance. We escalate our emotions to the point where our actions or words can be more damaging than the original offense.

This was at the lowest point in my life. I wanted justice in an unjust way. This was my condition when Mom became a Christian. I was the perfect picture of hopelessness!

PAUSE AND REFLECT
Read Romans 12:17-21

1. Are you struggling with an injustice and want to take matters into your own hands? Write about it.

2. Have you experienced a traumatic event that has thwarted your ability to see clearly? What was it? If this situation has not been dealt with, where can you start the healing process?

3. Can you trust God to avenge in His own way those that have wronged you? Why or why not?

The Mustard Seed

Mom changed as she grew in her faith. She became like her daughters Mary and Yvette. I would have teased her also, but I saw how happy she was. Mom was showing a side of her that I had never seen before—she was coming alive! Her relationship with Jesus and involvement in her church gave her a new purpose. She wasn't only living to work; she was living!

Mom wanted nothing more than her children to attend church with her. *If they could just hear the word, they will be saved.* Sometimes if there was a special speaker or event, I would go with her. I went forward at an altar call once, but it didn't have the same effect on me as it did for mom. Nothing changed and I continued the path I was on. This never stopped mom from praying for me.

"Let's pray in your daughter's room," the pastor's wife suggested during their usual prayer visit.

"Oh, it's a mess in there." Mom replied, unsure what condition my room would be in and hoping to avoid the embarrassment. Mom figured it didn't matter where they prayed and *God hears us out here.*

"No, we will pray in her room," the pastor's wife insisted. She wanted to enter enemy territory.

Mom complied. I cannot help but picture two women suiting up with the armor of God before entering my room. Mom understood spiritual warfare and the powers of this dark world. She knew her battle for me was in the spiritual realm.

The way to fight this kind of battle is through prayer by standing firm with the belt of truth, the breastplate of righteousness, the gospel of peace, the shield of faith, the helmet of salvation, and the sword of the Spirit, which is the word of God (Ephesians 6:14:17).

> "For our struggle is not against flesh and blood, but ... against the powers of this dark world and against the spiritual forces of evil ..." (Ephesians 6:12)

Jesus tells us we can move mountains with our prayers and all it requires is the faith of a mustard seed. Nothing will be impossible for us through prayer (Matthew 17:20-21). Yet, why is it that few of us accept the challenge of moving mountains with our mustard seed faith?

Scripture has many references to the way Jesus prayed. Jesus taught us to pray in The Lord's Prayer. He got up very early to pray and went to secluded places. He prayed up on a mountainside and prayed all night. He prayed for the deaf and mute man and he raised Lazarus from the dead with His prayer. He prayed before feeding both the crowds of 4000 and 5000 people. He prayed in the upper room, on the Mount of Olives and on the cross. He prayed for the children. He prayed for his disciples. He prayed specifically for Peter, and is praying for future believers—he prays for us!

Jesus' example helps us know how to pray, and if we don't know what to say, we are given the Holy Spirit as our intercessor. The Holy Spirit will pray on our behalf.

Mom and the pastor's wife moved a mountain that afternoon.

God heard their mustard seed prayer of faith and answered it just in time ...

PAUSE AND REFLECT
Read Ephesians 6:18

1. Describe your prayer life. Which parts resemble how Jesus prayed?

2. Do you pray out of obligation, habit, or to build a relationship with God?

3. When my children were young, I met with other moms to pray for our children. Who in your inner circle would pray with you?

After Some Time ...

"Jesus loves you," a stranger boldly told me during the lunch rush where I worked as a hostess.

"My mother believes in that stuff, but not me." I poured his coffee and didn't give his words another thought for the rest of my shift. It wasn't until I got home and changed out of my work clothes that I remembered this unusual interaction. "Jesus loves you." *Me?*

I had heard Jesus loves you a few times before this, however this day was different. Somehow these three words were bringing me to my knees. A different part of me heard it this time. I didn't hear some kind of challenge like, "change your life and get right with God." I heard Jesus loves *me*.

Those words didn't shame me into guilt; *I didn't need conviction in my life*. Rather, grace and mercy saturated those words—an expression of love I was beginning to understand. The simplicity of spiritual birth is that we are launched into our eternal journey as infants. I was a newborn, feeding on the Father's unconditional love for me—the, *I love you just the way you are* kind of love; the, *I don't deserve this* kind of love. It was true—I did nothing to earn it. I was an empty vessel being flooded from the inside out with the purest love ever to exist.

Like mom, I became the repentant woman at the feet of Jesus. I fell to my knees and wept that afternoon, and in the same way He called Lazarus to come forth from the grave, he called my name *Solé, come forth*. In my filthy rags I came to him. In my mess I surrendered my life. I was spiritually dead, and He resurrected me from this death to give me life.

My grave clothes fell off, and the stench of death lifted. Then the God of comfort filled me with the Holy Spirit and covered me in His righteousness. My life changed from that day forward.

Jesus is the resurrection and the life. He can resurrect even the hardest of hearts. No one is too far gone that He cannot reach them.

Thank you, Lord, for calling me out of the dark, cold grave. For sending someone to lift the heavy stone from my broken heart with three powerful words.

The message is simple: Jesus loves you and He's calling you by name to *come forth*!

> "... Believe in the Lord Jesus, and you will be saved—you and your household." (Acts 16:31)

7

A New Life

Praise be to the Lord, the God of Israel, because he has come to his people and redeemed them. (Luke 1:68)

A New Home

My family and I enjoyed watching the reality TV show *Extreme Home Makeover*. Ty Pennington, the host of this show, with his crew of designers and builders, would bless an unsuspecting family by presenting them with a complete home makeover along with an all expense paid vacation. The selected families were in dire need due to hardships—such as illness or a death in the family, resulting in neglected home maintenance and poor living conditions.

Watching this show often reminded me of *moving day* when I was young. Throughout my childhood, our family moved often. It had nothing to do with my parents' jobs; it had to do with dysfunction in the home. I suspect my parents were evicted for not paying the rent, as most of their arguing revolved around money.

Sometimes I would come home from school to find that

our power was shut off or phone disconnected. We learned to adapt by taking quick, cold showers. When my parents decided it was time to move, we had one day to pack our belongings. They didn't give us much warning to say goodbye to our friends at school.

Moving day was a chance to leave things behind, hoping for something better ahead. My siblings and I learned to make the best of things. I found it to be an adventure to enter the *new* house we were moving into, very much like the children's reactions you'd see on Extreme Home Makeover. We were like children on a sugar buzz, bouncing from room to room, trying to see who could get through the fastest. We explored every inch of the place, opening closets and kitchen cupboards. "This is my room!" I would yell and quickly put my belongings in it before my siblings would beat me to it. A different house provided new hiding spots for a fresh game of hide and seek. The excitement of moving into a new house came from the possibility of a fresh start. *Maybe my parents won't fight in this house.*

The climax of the Extreme Home Makeover was when the renovated house was about to be revealed. The only thing keeping the family from entering their home was a motor coach bus parked in front of the house blocking the view. To get the bus out of the way, those gathered for the reveal would yell, "Driver, move that bus!" As the bus slowly drove away, the camera honed in on the family's reaction to their new beginnings. I have shed a few tears as I watched them enter their new home and go from room to room in full humility and gratitude.

Likewise, Jesus offers us a complete life makeover, renovating our life from the inside out. We can leave our old life behind in anticipation of a new one ahead as we *move* towards Him.

> "I will give you a new heart and put a new spirit in you; I will remove from you your heart of stone and give you a heart of flesh. And I will put my Spirit in you and move you to follow my decrees and be careful to keep my laws." (Ezekiel 36:26-27)

God, Jesus, and the Holy Spirit are at work renewing us from the inside out. God replaces the old with something new. We are like the tattered run-down house that God wants to restore! He has detailed plans and a clear vision of our life and purpose. The best part is that God will never stop working on us. *I am grateful for God's ongoing work in me.*

The climax of our story is when we see God face to face and hear him say, "Well done, good and faithful servant" (Matthew 25:23)! It is then that we get to move into our eternal home—the one Jesus has been preparing for us (John 14:2-3).

PAUSE AND REFLECT
Read Philippians 1:6

1. What is something you wish to leave behind?

2. In what area of your life do you desire a new beginning?

3. What fresh starts have you experienced from God's work? Do you trust that God will complete the *good work* in you?

4. Through Jesus, we have a second chance. Within healthy boundaries, how do you feel about offering others a second chance?

A New Family

"Do not love the world or anything in the world. If anyone loves the world, love for the Father is not in them. For everything in the world—the lust of the flesh, the lust of the eyes, and the pride of life—comes not from the Father but from the world. The world and its desires pass away, but whoever does the will of God lives forever." (1 John 2:15-17)

This was the first verse I memorized when I became a Christian. It reminded me that I no longer belonged to the world. I found a new love and committed my life to Him. My focus was to learn about Jesus. I hungered for the Word and read it at every opportunity. This changed my life.

Jesus rescues us and redeems us. He changes our heart and worldview. Then, with fresh eyes we look at our life*style* and see things that need to change, things that we want to change, things that He is inviting us to change. For some, it can feel like a lot. It was my love for Jesus that prompted me to allow changes in my life.

Disconnecting from my old life meant a new way of living—letting go of destructive habits, and even my best friend Alicia who was like a sister to me. This coming to Christ is a willingness to leave houses, brothers, sisters, fathers, mothers, spouses, and children for His sake. The promise is that we receive a hundred times as much, and will inherit eternal life (Matthew 19:29).

We receive a new family—a family in the faith. Even so, it broke my heart, and I prayed that Alicia would know Jesus the way I did and join me on this amazing journey. It doesn't always work out this way. We stayed in touch but never hung out the way we used to. We are still friends and my love for her remains unchanged.

Just as I had seen mom do, I sought people who would help me grow in my faith. I needed to connect with a church, the body of Christ.

The first church I attended taught me a valuable lesson early in my faith. Everyone seemed put together. I was not. Maybe I was overdressed or underdressed. Maybe my tears made those around me feel uncomfortable. Perhaps people noticed my lagging baggage and didn't want to help me unpack it. I felt judged and alone—though perhaps I was simply judging myself. Either way, I felt out of place. I didn't look the part—whatever I thought that *look* should be. I didn't speak Christianese—the words we learn after being in the church for a few years. I was a sinner saved by grace, trying to find my place.

At this specific church, no one greeted me. *Maybe going to church isn't right for me.* It would have been easy not to go back to another church, but my hunger kept me in the race. I can see how people can disconnect because of a lack of genuine community. It takes courage for someone, especially a new believer, to go to church alone.

While in church, let's make an effort to greet and engage with newcomers. Let them know you are glad they are there.

We don't know why they showed up—what they are seeking. Connect outside of the church building with someone who may be hurting, lonely, or confused. Let us never be *too busy* to meet with someone in need.

Jesus set an example for us as He made sure not to be *too busy*, as the Father booked his schedule with divine appointments such as the one with the woman at the well.

Jesus went out of his way to meet the Samaritan woman. He broke cultural barriers for this divine appointment. You can find this story in John chapter 4.

> "You are a Jew and I am a Samaritan woman. How can you ask me for a drink?" (For Jews do not associate with Samaritans (v.9).)

That afternoon encounter with Jesus changed this woman's life. Not only that, Scripture tells us "many of the Samaritans from that town believed in Him because of the woman's testimony" (v. 39).

She unashamedly told the people in her town, "He (Jesus) told me everything I ever did." She immediately began sharing her *if people knew* testimony, which caused others to seek Jesus.

> So when the Samaritans came to him, they urged him to stay with them, and he stayed two days. And because of his words, many more became believers (vv. 40-41).

This detour in Jesus' journey changed an entire community.

You may think, *but I am not Jesus*. Yes, this is correct, but to some people, we are the only glimpse of Jesus they will see.

Allow detours and welcome interruptions. Look at the world through the eyes of Christ, and share what He has done for you—your *if people knew* testimony. People are hungry for this personal message. People are hungry for the truth.

I became a member of a different church, got baptized, and made some new friends. These friends have traveled the healing journey with me and have joyfully celebrated my redemption. My children, husband, and I have been included in their prayers. These friends know my, *if people knew*, story and have loved me anyway. These are the friends that have become my family in the faith.

PAUSE AND REFLECT
Read John 4

1. Are you thinking of detours in your day as divine appointments God has planned for you? Write about one detour that had a favorable outcome.

2. Who have you left because of your new life in Christ?

3. Do you share life with other believers in the faith? What does Hebrews 10:24-25 ask us to consider?

4. What is your level of involvement with the local church?

A New Job

With my new faith came the realization that I had to leave the job I had as a hostess. I did not want to go back to my old life so I intentionally established healthy boundaries for myself and leaving this job was my first move. I also began to dream again, and these dreams did not include being in the restaurant business. I wanted something else—I just wasn't sure what, or how to go about it.

For as long as I could remember I wanted to help people. In my early teens, while my friends read Teen Beat magazines, I subscribed to Psychology Today. I spent hours in the public library digging into books from the great minds of psychology such as Freud, Jung, and Skinner. I was hungry for knowledge. I wanted to understand human behavior and thought that these *experts* might hold the key to show me how to navigate life's difficulties. I yearned to know how to overcome my psychological challenges and help others do the same.

Because my family moved often, and I attended many schools, I felt like I was always trying to catch up academically. This angered me because I love learning. I fed this desire by reading the Encyclopedia Britannica collection mom kept in a bookcase at home. The idea of going to college was not brought up at our house. Mom figured if her children could graduate from high school, they would be further along than she was. As I got older, I lost sight of the vision I had to become a psychologist. I had no hope of pursuing a college degree because I was convinced it was not possible. This is what the voice of shame says. *People like you won't ever…* it says; *Someone like you can't ...*

So there I was, a new believer at seventeen years old, removing myself from my old life and transitioning into my new life without a job. I did the next best thing available: I applied with a temporary agency that matches you up with companies seeking short-term employees. Based on the evaluation, my strengths pointed to clerical/secretarial type work.

They sent me to an investment company to fill in for someone who was on maternity leave. The job was auditing large accounts and reconciling them. I don't know how they trusted me with this financial responsibility other than God's hand was behind it. To my surprise, I cleaned up accounts in record time. They sent me to another department that needed help, and I excelled there as well. The favor of God was upon me (Psalms 90:17). He was doing that *good work* in my life. After many months as a temp, they hired me full time.

This company paid for my extended education in the insurance and investment field. My love for learning rekindled like wildfire and is still aflame. I took all the classes the company offered. This led to promotions and more responsibility during my time there. The pay was just as good as if I had a college degree. Thank you, Jesus! To this day it has been one of my favorite jobs, and was the best company I have ever worked for.

God gave me what I needed at just the right time. Even though it wasn't in the field of helping others in the way I longed for in my earlier years, my redemption story was just beginning. And just like yours, it is still being written.

PAUSE AND REFLECT
Read Psalms 90:17

1. Are you willing to take risks, leave your job, church, friends, and grow in your faith as God directs? If not, what or who is holding you back?

2. What did you aspire to be as a child? Write about some of those childhood dreams.

3. In what ways have you sabotaged potential successes in your life?

4. Where have you seen evidence of God's favor in your life?

A New Future

Mom brought the blond-haired, blue-eyed neighbor she wanted to match me up with over to our apartment. With her heavy Spanish accent, she could barely say his name "Duane" properly, so instead she called him "the American boy." Duane lived in the townhouse right across from ours. I could see his unit from my bedroom window.

Mom was persistent. She had an intuition about these things. At first, I was not interested. I was growing and learning to live out my new faith. I didn't want any distractions. I was a woman on a mission, ready to go to the most remote areas of the Earth to serve my God.

"Here am I. Send me!" (Isaiah. 6:8)

What I didn't know was that "the American boy" had experienced the Holy Spirit's prompting when he confessed Jesus as his savior during chapel at the Christian high school he attended. He had started on the same path as me, but the popularity as a talented high school athlete diverted him from his faith.

I couldn't get away from mom or Duane (not that I was trying) and eventually let my guard down and got to know him. We would sit on the steps outside my front door and talk for hours in the evenings. Almost every morning he would place notes folded tightly to fit under my car door handle. He made me feel special and pursued me daily. I let my guard down and allowed him in.

I was the girl next door; he was Mr. Wright. Duane won me over and I fell in love with him. After a few months of dating, we were married. We were two young, broken adults trying to figure out life and faith with God by our side.

We vowed to commit our lives to each other, and to our God. This doesn't mean our marriage has not struggled or that we have been problem free. In our flesh, we will always mess up. We know tough times come into every marriage, and they certainly have for us. However, God has been the glue that has kept us together all these years. As Christians, we show the world that all things are possible with God.

Early in our marriage we became involved in ministry by teaching Sunday School and discipleship programs. Duane was a part of the men's ministry which met every Saturday morning at our church in Florida We were *doing*! We were making God proud! Everything was falling into place. There was consistency and normalcy in my life—something I had hungered for in my early years.

I believed as long as I was committed to my faith and *doing* God's work, life would go well for me. *I have suffered enough; God is going to give me a successful life now.*

The Christian life is not a fairy tale, with a happily ever after narrative. This was a distorted view of my early Christian faith. There is a difference between *happily ever after* and *after some time*.

PAUSE AND REFLECT
Read Jeremiah 29:11-14

1. Write about an unplanned situation and its outcome.

2. What distorted views have you had about your role as a Christian and your expectations of God?

3. What does Jeremiah 29:11 say about God's plans for you? Do you believe this?

4. What does God want from us? (vv.12-13)

A New Heart

It had been over thirty years since I last saw Oscar. There he was, an aged man, slowly walking into the funeral home to pay his respects—vulnerable in a sort of way. Mom's viewing was not a place for only those who deserved to be there. Everyone needs closure in their own way.

As was the norm, we kept our distance and there was never an exchange of words between us, but seeing him triggered me. A few days after mom's funeral, I had a nightmare so terrifying that my husband had to wake me up from it. It had been decades since I had experienced something that sparked such an intense reaction. I had almost forgotten about this part of trauma.

> Triggers: the unfriendly reminder of what we have survived.

I don't know if my triggers will ever be fully gone, although they are now less frequent. Sometimes repeated triggers can stem from underlying unforgiveness. It is important to recognize that forgiving an offender is a choice we must consider in order to move forward in our personal healing.

There was a time when forgiving Oscar seemed impossible. I wrestled with this struggle most of my life. *I need to forgive, but can't, won't, don't want to* ... Unforgiveness held the spotlight over what was done, confining me to the past. I prayed for the supernatural ability to forgive, and ... nothing happened.

No matter how many books I read or sermons I listened to on forgiveness, I couldn't forgive—I was stuck!

Then, when I thought I had forgiven, I realized anger was still present. This anger kept me trapped as a victim to the past. I've had to unpack this part of my story countless times to release it once and for all. I had to realize that my past abuse has no hold on my life today. I am no longer living that life.

I knew what Jesus said:

> "For if you forgive other people when they sin against you, your heavenly Father will also forgive you. But if you do not forgive others their sins, your Father will not forgive your sins." (Matthew 6:14-15)

Yes, I knew what Jesus asked of me concerning forgiveness, and I needed and wanted God's forgiveness in my life. Yet it was so difficult to let go of my step-father's actions against me.

Forgiving doesn't mean we have to maintain a relationship with the offender or excuse their behavior. It doesn't mean we forget the offense—that is nearly impossible! Forgiveness releases the grip of the person and the offense it has on you.

I have shared how forgiveness shone a light into my relationship with my mother as we both entered this act together—how it freed us from the past and deepened our relationship. Forgiveness is a powerful act that will set you (and in some situations the offender) free—just as it did for my biological father.

Forgiveness came with the help of the Holy Spirit and the

realization that I am a sinner, just like my offender.

Even though our *sins* differ, Jesus' death was for all sins—even what we consider to be big or small like "little white lies." We are all sinners and fall short of the glory of God (Romans 3:23).

I choose to forgive because I need the forgiveness of my heavenly Father (Luke 6:37, Colossians 3:13). I choose to forgive because I do not want my prayers hindered (Mark 11:25). I choose to forgive because I want others to forgive me when I sin against them. Unforgiveness was too heavy of a burden to carry, and forgiveness lifted the load. This *choosing* is difficult, it's an ongoing struggle of wanting justice but surrendering the situation to God.

People do awful things out of their own pain and trauma. I know I have. I have hurt myself because of my pain and have hurt those I love the most from this same pain. Perhaps this is Oscar's story, and he acted out on it. I don't know. Mom once told me that Oscar became a Christian. I hope this is true. I pray God redeems Oscar's life as He has redeemed mine.

> Jesus said, "Father, forgive them, for they do not know what they are doing." (Luke 23:34)

Thank you Jesus for the cross, for advocating to the Father on our behalf and for modeling forgiveness.

PAUSE AND REFLECT
Read Matthew 18:21-35

1. Are you aware of what triggers you?

2. Have you forgiven those who have hurt you? How many times does Jesus want you to forgive them? Perhaps this repetition is the process towards complete forgiveness.

3. Express what it means to be forgiven by Jesus.

4. Is unforgiveness hindering the work of the Holy Spirit in your life?

After Some Time ...

Upon my salvation, God immediately took away the hold drugs and alcohol had on me. This was the part of my *unpacking* that He took charge of. There are things that God instantaneously removes from our life that are just too much for us to do on our own. Consider asking God to remove what you cannot do on your own and to help you sort and dump the other things that are weighing you down.

I've spent the last few decades sorting and dumping. This work has been for my benefit in order to mature me. I've thrown away things that had a grasp on me, like unforgiveness, things that don't serve God's purpose in my life. Getting rid of unnecessary baggage creates space for the plans God has set for me.

In comparison to my childhood, today, there is stability in my life. I have been living in the same house for over twenty-three years. That is the external evidence of stability, but the stability in the heart—the renovation that happened on the inside—is what's even more important and what will carry me into eternity. That internal stability helps Duane and me get through tough times together. I know without a doubt that God was the real matchmaker over 34 years ago.

God has given us abundant life—not full of material possessions, but full of the richness of love, faith, and family. We have raised four children and are now in the joys of grand parenting. Perfect life? Not at all. Redeemed life? Absolutely!

The path I am on has also allowed me to help others overcome challenges. I realize it wasn't so much that I aspired to be a psychologist; it was more about coming alongside others on their redemptive journey.

What is God inviting you to do? Is it time to take a peek inside your baggage? Is it a new move, a new job, or perhaps time to find a new church? None of these moves are easy; just know that you are not moving alone.

8

Surrender

This is what the LORD says—your Redeemer, who formed you in the womb: I am the LORD, the Maker of all things ...
(Isaiah 44:24)

Running

AT AGE TWENTY-THREE, MY friend Dianne invited me to join her on a Saturday run with her running club. Until then, I had never taken part in an organized sport or considered myself athletic, although I have always exercised for health and fitness.

During gym class in school, I was frequently the last person to be chosen for a team. When Dianne asked me to join the club, I felt honored and went all in. *Someone picked me to join their team!*

I didn't know the running club was training for an upcoming marathon. I was unaware of what the eight-mile run would entail, which was the plan for that morning. I don't remember if she told me, and it may not have mattered. All I knew was to be ready by 5:30 a.m. I entered this team, this running club, blindly.

To my surprise, I ran that morning with energy to spare, still unaware of the fact that I had just completed eight miles on my first run ever. The following Saturday was ten miles—also not a problem. I learned that I have natural endurance for distance running and fell in love with it. Before you become too impressed with my running skills, my runs were at a jogging pace—I was not a fast runner. This was not something that bothered me, since I never developed a competitive nature. I just enjoyed my runs—um, jogs.

Running became a part of my identity. It was also my escape, a stress reliever, my drug of choice. It gave me energy to get through the day and lifted my mood. Running also became an addiction.

My runs were often very early in the morning before my children woke up. As they got older, I began running longer distances and eventually signed up for races. I spent countless hours hitting the pavement during my training runs. I listened to audiobooks, podcasts, praise songs and even prayed during those hours.

As time went on, I decided to run a marathon in each state. This became my empty nester's bucket list goal, and 2020 was to be the year this dream would become a reality. I signed up for The Grandma Marathon in Minnesota and The Flying Pig Marathon in Ohio. I was weight training and felt the strongest I had been in a long time. Physically and mentally, I was ready to live out this dream.

Sometimes we make plans or dream dreams for our future in a season of our life where it may seem fitting. We don't consider the possibility that life will take a different turn, or that our plans do not align with what God has for us.

I didn't know this then, but God had other plans for me. I believe He needed to slow me down. To get rid of what came easily so that I would learn to *lean on Him* during the hard stuff that was to come.

PAUSE AND REFLECT
Read Proverbs 19:21

1. Recall a time when you were *picked*. How did this make you feel?

2. What are some of your bucket list dreams? Could this dream interfere with what God wants to do through you?

3. Could your natural talents—what comes easy—be preventing you from what God has called you to do? Are you running from God or running towards Him?

4. Write about a time you entered into something blindly, and it worked out for you.

The Setback

In March 2020, some of my family members and I contracted COVID on a trip to Strasburg, Virginia. We were celebrating my daughter Megan's graduation from Officer Candidate School with the Marines. This was the weekend in March when everything shut down because of the virus.

I was visibly sick for about five weeks. The obvious symptoms were fatigue, muscle weakness, difficulty breathing, and a complete loss of my sense of smell. It was well over a year until I regained my sense of smell.

My post-Covid condition made it impossible for me to run a mile. My doctor didn't understand my prolonged symptoms of chronic fatigue, shortness of breath, and heart palpitations. Medical professionals were just learning about this virus and the side effects from it. Today we know I was experiencing long-haulers syndrome. All my doctor offered was antidepressants, which I didn't think was the cure. I knew depression, and this was not it. I left her office frustrated and confused about what was going on in my body.

Over the course of a year, my resting heart rate remained constantly elevated. I lost both muscle mass and twenty pounds. My hair was falling off in clumps. I tried living life as normally as possible, hiding my hand tremors by holding on to my hands or sitting on them. I was trying to figure things out on my own and didn't want others to know that I, a person who promotes health and fitness, was falling apart. *I should have all this figured out. I shouldn't be struggling with poor health. I am a fake.* I was faced with either continuing in my pride and figuring things out on my own or humbling myself by asking for help.

Isn't this a common default for most of us? We pretend we are not fighting a battle inside. We don't want others to know our struggles because we will seem weak. Pride ... perhaps?

I also began suffering from what I will call, "spiritual long-haulers," chronic symptoms that develop after many years of being complacent in the Christian faith. I have seen that the longer some people are in the faith, the more difficult it can be to show weakness. We believe we cannot share our struggles because of our position in the church, ministry, or profession. We cannot admit defeat in an area of our life because we have *walked with the Lord for decades*. We separate ourselves from community and from hearing God's voice. Definitely pride!

Life is full of curveballs and only Jesus has the skills to catch every single one of them. This is where I was finding myself—between dodging the balls thrown at me and allowing Jesus to take over. I was a wrestling with pride and humility, when all I had to do was just surrender.

> **PAUSE AND REFLECT**
> **Read 2 Corinthians 12:7-10**

1. Are you more concerned with the image of a "good Christian" or being more Christlike?

2. What is the "thorn in your side" that God has allowed in your life? Is His power being made perfect in this weakness? Allow God to use your weakness in order that He may be glorified with whatever the outcome may be. This is a bold prayer of faith.

3. What situations in your daily life make you feel out of control?

Keep Knocking

As my symptoms continued, I began the search for another doctor. Dr. Leslie came highly recommended, however, she was not taking new patients. Based on the recommendations, I *knew* this doctor could help me. I refused to accept the fact that she was not taking new patients as a closed door, so I kept knocking. Every so often I would call her office, asking, "Is Dr. Leslie taking new patients now?" *After some time*, the door opened, and I booked an appointment. I wonder if the office staff became annoyed over my persistence. *Let's just get her in because she will call back next week!* This appointment was almost a year after my symptoms began.

At my first appointment, Dr. Leslie gave me undivided attention and listened without interruption. I knew I was in the right place and was going to get answers.

After many tests, it was determined that COVID had activated an immune response in my body. So my body turned on itself, very much like I had been doing for most of my life—self-sabotage. We often do that, turn on ourselves, don't we?

"Have you experienced any childhood trauma?" Dr. Leslie asked.

"Yes. Haven't we all?"

"It is common for people with childhood trauma to develop autoimmune disease. I recommend seeing Dr. Beeman, who specializes in EMDR. Would you be interested in seeing her?"

"Yes!" I figured, *why not*?

During this time I was writing a book on negative thought

patterns and found myself *stuck* in the writing process. Perhaps there was a connection to what my body and mind were experiencing.

Despite years of personal growth, counseling, and my relationship with God, I still struggled with the *dead inside* feeling from my childhood. This would be the perfect opportunity to uncover this mystery.

PAUSE AND REFLECT
Read Matthew 7:7-11

1. Where do you need to persevere—to keep knocking?

2. What are you still struggling with that you thought by now you would have overcome?

3. How are your listening skills? Do you interrupt to get a word in before you forget? Do you change the topic or do you check out?

4. Do you remain still enough to listen to the voice of God?

The Redirection

Dr. Beeman had a long waiting list. I was willing to wait, and four months later, I scheduled my first appointment.

As with all first appointments, we went through introductions. She had questions for me about what my goals were during our time together. I told her about my "stuck, dead inside" feeling as I pointed to my gut in a swirling motion with my hand. She made a note of that.

I was not familiar with EMDR. She explained it and I still didn't understand it fully. For those that do not know, I got this definition from the website she recommended:

> Eye Movement Desensitization and Reprocessing (EMDR) therapy is an extensively researched, effective psychotherapy method proven to help people recover from trauma and PTSD symptoms. EMDR is a structured therapy that encourages the patient to briefly focus on the trauma memory while simultaneously experiencing bilateral stimulation (typically eye movements), which is associated with a reduction in the vividness and emotion associated with the trauma memories. EMDR therapy does not require talking in detail about the distressing issue or completing homework between sessions. EMDR therapy, rather than focusing on changing the emotions, thoughts, or behaviors resulting from the distressing issue, allows the brain to

resume its natural healing process. EMDR therapy is designed to resolve unprocessed traumatic memories in the brain.[1]

Dr. Beeman provided three stimulating options—the light-bar, the hand sensors, and the headphones. She recommended we use two of the three during the EMDR session.

The light bar is a few feet long in width. It sits on a tripod in front of you at eye level. It has a red light that navigates from left to right at an adjustable speed, according to what feels right for you.

The vibrating hand sensors, small enough to fit in each hand, are also adjustable to the strength and speed of the vibration that feels comfortable for you.

The headphones provide a beeping tone, which bounces from one ear to the other. The headphone is also adjustable for speed and volume. All these stimulating options work in unison with one another.

We decided what topic of my childhood we would discuss first—my most disturbing memory. I figured I'd work on the obvious ones, which revolved around Oscar. We touched on these memories for a few months. I discovered that I still wrestled with low-self image and more healing needed to take place. After a few months, we seemed to have worked through my childhood traumatic events, but one remained: my mother's attempts to abort me.

I had planned to do some research on this topic for my negative thought patterns book. I wondered if I had trauma from before birth *if this was really a thing*. I told Dr. Beeman I would see what information I could find. I wanted to reach out to others who survived abortion attempts and ask if they also experienced these same confusing emotions.

Were they stuck like me? Did they feel dead inside?

I had seen the movie *October Baby*, the story of Gianna Jessen who was born after a failed abortion, when it came out in 2012.[2] While watching this movie, I shut down emotionally when she described feelings of drowning in her journal. There was something there, but I was too afraid to enter this part of my story back then.

After deciding we were going to do EMDR on my next visit regarding my *dead inside* feelings, I went home and began my research.

To my surprise, I discovered that there are more people like me. I found The Abortion Survivors Network and wrote them an email asking if someone could contact me regarding research for a book I was working on. In that email I was not ready to disclose that I was in counseling. For some reason, I was in denial that this pre-birth part of my life had an adverse effect on me. I sent my email and waited for someone to respond.

A week later I had my appointment with Dr. Beeman and we began working on this part of my story. I still had not spoken with anyone at The Abortion Survivors Network.

Since I hadn't been born yet, I had to go by the stories I was told by Mom, step-father, and biological father. I decided to use the headphones along with the hand sensors in each hand this time. I was relaxed and ready to enter this specific story I had been told. I visually went there as I had done a few times in the past.

I saw mom enter the bathroom and close the door. As she took off her clothes, I could see the baby bump. She reached for the faucet to turn the water on and after checking the water temperature she entered the bathtub. Facing the running water, she squatted and began to get rid of the problem—me.

This has been the part in my mind where I always saw blood. I tell Dr. Beeman I am feeling pressure on the top of my head. (I know about this pressure because I asked her for the notes of this session. I don't recall saying this.) Beep, left. Beep, right. The hand vibrations, bzzt bzzt, were flowing, left to right.

Mom slowly disappears, as if she is becoming invisible. I no longer see her, but the womb. The baby bump is the only thing visible. The backdrop remains the same, in the bathtub. I see a baby in a womb, existing in midair, and water flowing from the faucet.

The pressure in my head remains and now I begin to breathe heavily (Dr. Beeman's notes). Beep beep. Bzzt bzzt.

Suddenly two large powerful hands appear. The hands begin reaching for the womb, for me. Each hand was on either side of the womb, holding it in place. Then the left hand continues moving towards the cervix and cups its fingers over it. As the left hand is reaching for the cervix, I hear these words. "I will fight for you. I will fight for you. I will fight for you."

I took a deep breath.

With both hands in position, holding onto me, protecting me, I hear, "I didn't create you for your mother. I created you for myself. I will protect you. Nothing can snatch you out of my hands. You are mine."

Beep beep. Bzzt bzzt. Tears are streaming down my face.

"I didn't create you for your mother. I created you for myself. You are fearfully and wonderfully made."

The stuck feeling was miraculously gone. For the first time in my life, I felt fully alive, complete. At fifty-one years old, I finally understood what "I am fearfully and wonderfully made" meant. (Psalms 139:14)

Dr. Beeman told me at one point my hands pressed against the top of my head. I didn't realize this. My body was holding on to this trauma. It remembered what was done to it.

Through this experience, I saw the depth of God's love for me. He was there, and fought for my life. Perhaps this was when my biological father entered the bathroom and pulled mom out of the tub. God always put someone in my life to preserve it.

I have learned that God speaks to us in different ways. He is a personal God, and as we read throughout Scriptures we see that He gives people what they need in order to draw them closer to Him, to get their attention, and to heal them. Each person gets something unique.

I received another gift from God that day. During that time, I had to draw blood on a monthly basis to monitor my numbers because of the autoimmune disease. Before I left Dr. Beeman's office, I knew my next blood work, which was that day, would come back normal. It did! This experience completely healed me.

If God can part the Red Sea, speak through a donkey, allow Sarah to conceive past the age of childbearing, shut the lion's mouth keeping Daniel safe, provide bread from heaven, feed thousands with very little food, raise the dead, turn water into wine, and walk on water, shouldn't we be on the lookout for miracles? God has no limits. We should not set our expectations of God according to our own limitations.

> "For my thoughts are not your thoughts, neither are your ways my ways," declares the LORD. "As the heavens are higher than the earth, so are my ways higher than your ways and my thoughts than your thoughts." (Isaiah 55:8-9)

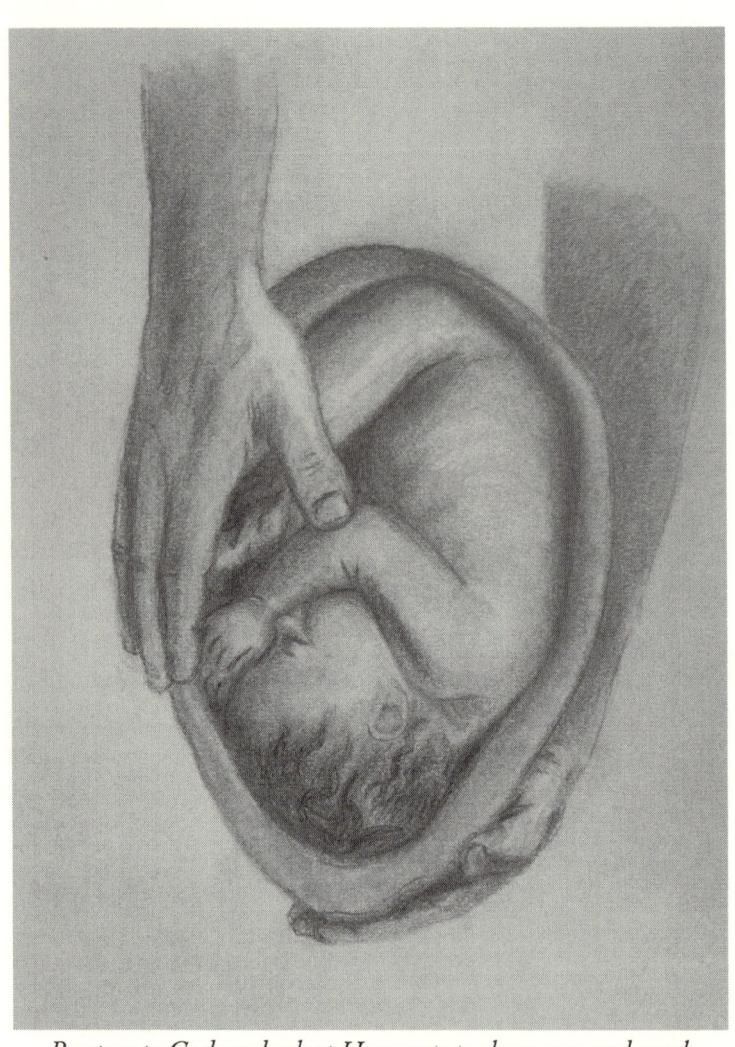

Be open to God and what He wants to show you and work through you. You are in His hands.

PAUSE AND REFLECT
Read Matthew 28:1-10

1. Reflecting on your own life, where has God consistently shown up?

2. Are you on the lookout for miracles? If not, ask God to reveal to you through scripture His omnipotence.

3. Do you believe God created you for Himself and are set aside for His purpose?

4. In Matthew 28 we read the miracle of all miracles, the resurrection of Jesus, the foundation of our Christian faith. Spend time in praise and gratitude for Jesus' willingness to give His life for yours.

The Retreat

"The plane just landed. I will call you when I get to the ranch." I sent Duane the text and gathered my bag from the overhead bin. What I thought was going to be research for a book turned out to be a weekend trip to Schulenberg, Texas. *How did one phone call get me signed up to a retreat with people I have never met and with an organization I never knew existed?*

Four days after the breakthrough with Dr. Beeman, I received the phone call.

"Hi, Solé, this is Robin Sertell from The Abortion Survivors Network."

Robin is a saline abortion survivor and the author of *Miracles Happen in the Wilderness: A Story of Remembrance.*[3]

"I would like to tell you a bit about who we are, about myself, and how I can help you with your book."

My conversation with Robin extended into my healing journey. She shared her story with me and I shared mine with her. She validated both my feelings and my autoimmune disease.

"A lot of abortion survivors have health issues, autoimmune in nature. A lot of survivors have received visions surrounding their prenatal state and/or birth and have a strong faith in God."

We spoke for about an hour. At the end of the conversation, she asked how she could help me with my book. The book was the last thing on my mind.

For the second time that week, I was unexpectedly blown away. Speaking with someone that I could resonate with on this specific topic was a gift to me. Robin also told me about an upcoming retreat that would take place at the end of the month. *What are the chances of a retreat within weeks of a very specific major breakthrough?* God was in all of this.

At the retreat, I expressed without shame or hesitation how a part of me felt dead inside. I shared *the secret that kept me stuck*—the secret I believed no one would understand. I shared this with faith-based women. Even though this organization is not faith-based, most members have a personal relationship with Jesus. I felt safe, and knew that not one of them would question my faith or my experience. They understood because they'd had similar emotions surrounding their own stories.

While sharing, I made eye contact with Priscilla, a lovely woman who was also an abortion survivor. She went through an abortion herself, and worked as a nurse at an abortion clinic. She simply nodded yes as I was expressing what I had felt inside. I knew she understood. There was a sacredness surrounding the stories told and the way they ministered to our spirits.

Meeting and speaking with others who understood my deepest secret convinced me that I am not alone. No one is. It was yet another confirmation of our *need* for one another.

After the retreat, I realized I had to write my story. My *after some time* story of redemption. I set aside the book I was writing on negative thought patterns and poured my heart into this one. I want you to know you are not alone in whatever storyline you are finding yourself in. There are others like you. The only way to know who the *others* are is to share your story.

"Let the redeemed of the LORD tell their story—" (Psalms 107:2)

PAUSE AND REFLECT
Read Ephesians 3:14-20

1. How difficult is it to wait on the Lord? Write about a time you waited and God came through for you. How was the timing?

2. Would you be willing to hold your plans loosely and let God make changes as He guides you?

3. What has God redeemed in your life by your obedience to Him?

After Some Time …

I was in my thirties when I entered this healing journey and began to notice God's redemptive nature within my story. There were times I thought I would not see restoration on this side of heaven. Yet, He remained faithful and mended my brokenness and relationships beyond my expectations.

My goal to run a marathon in every state is no longer on my list. Making this decision was tough, as it meant the death of a dream. Letting go of dreams that don't align with God's purpose is necessary. In doing so, we make room for God's leading and His plans. This goal distracted me from my family and from God's calling—it was all about me. Releasing this dream brought me back to the one God placed in my heart when my children were young—sharing my redemptive story.

I am thankful to God, my family, friends, and a therapist for their role in my journey. Difficult life situations require support from others, including professionals, in order to overcome them. God has gifted people with wisdom and skills to guide those who are suffering. This overcoming is possible for anyone who wants it and does the work involved.

Today I am living the future I never thought possible—the one I was *holding on* for when I wanted out. This change was the result of unraveling my story and running to God with it. The trials life has given me have also changed me. I have grown through the continuous knocking, the persevering, the seeking God with all my heart even when He has felt distant.

As we come to a close, I want you to grasp the truth that you are not alone in whatever situation you may find yourself in.

Never forget that God created you for Himself and He will fight for you. He has plans for your life. You can take Him at His Word because it never fails. He is the great Redeemer!

Be on the lookout for your *after some time* testimony and share it with others.

Epilogue

I can't believe I am this close to fulfilling my dream of writing a book!

This was the thought running through my mind the day tragic events would take me from my mountaintop of praise to the valley of pain once again. I was in the proofreading phase of this book and had ended it with soaring encouragement about how God is the great Redeemer, no matter what life brings your way.

A split-second moment—a tragic car crash—has now brought unexpected and new heartache so that my quest for redemption continues. In my humanness, I can't see how anything good can come out of what took place on that day. No matter how hard I try to make sense of it and find the silver lining, it is not there. Then again, it has only been six weeks since it happened. The pain is still quite raw.

Yet, I know my God, and He *is* good. Nothing happens in my life unless it has passed through his hands. The hands that created and protected me in the womb are the same hands holding me right now. Understanding what He is working out in my life and in the life of others involved is not within my control.

It is up to me to lean on Him and believe that He has not left me nor forsaken me during this difficult time (Deuteronomy 31:6). It is up to me to keep my eyes fixed on Jesus, the pioneer and perfecter of my faith, and to continue the race that is set before me (Hebrews 12:2). It is up to me to grab ahold of His hands, where my story unfolds, and never let go.

In this brokenness, I have contemplated giving up on this book. The voices coming at me during this low point in my life are saying, *Nobody cares about what you have to say. Do you really want everyone to know all this about you? It won't make a difference.*

When you feel like giving up, I want to encourage you in the waiting—when redemption has not yet come. It is in this waiting room that I am sitting in right now and selfishly praying to speak with someone that has gone ahead of me.

Even though I know I am not alone, I *feel* like I am.

My usual morning routine involves getting a cup of coffee, sitting on the couch by the soft light of a lamp on an end table, and reading my Bible. This is often followed by prayer and listening to a sermon. When my children were young, if they woke up earlier than usual they would quietly snuggle beside me until I finished. I treasured those moments. These days it is my husband and me—and still very special.

There was something different about my prayer that morning. There was a distinct sense of confirmation in my soul that my prayer was heard. In a childlike manner, I remember feeling giddy. *My Father hears me!* This prayer was prompted by a session at a recent weeklong Biblical Counseling Training I attended. The topic focused on idols of the heart. During the conference, I was convicted on how I always put my children first and now my grandbabies have taken the front row in my life. It made me wonder what other things or people have my heart above God.

"Lord, show me my idols. Reveal to me what is in my heart."

I am uncertain if what happened that day was in response to that prayer, if it pertains to my current struggles, or if it still remains undisclosed. Only *after some time* and continued prayers, will it be revealed.

Up to that day, after my morning devotionals, I typically exercised for about thirty minutes. That morning after finishing my kettlebell workout, I had a private celebration. It had taken me forty-five days to perfect this specific routine. Yes! The muscle tone I lost after my autoimmune disease diagnosis had returned. Even better, month after month, my blood work continued to come back normal—which could only mean I had been in remission for over a year. I could feel and see the difference. Once again, with new knowledge, I was ready to support others on their health journey.

My plan was to create workout videos, such as the kettlebell routine, with the goal of launching a spring bootcamp for wellness on my coaching app. The app was out of the beta testing and I already had a coaching client.

So far, two wins for the day and the best was yet to come—time with the grandbabies!

On a typical Thursday, I would run errands, have lunch with my daughter and grandchildren, and spend the afternoon with them. And yes, it was another win. We had a great day!

At a stop sign on my way home, I asked myself, *Do I go home or go look for the eyedrops I couldn't find earlier? Turn left and go home or turn right and go back into town to get the drops?* Everything about that day was so vivid and memorable, even the conversations that took place in my head. I turned right to get the eye drops. This was the split second decision that changed everything.

As I crested a hill—a vehicle was in my lane, leaving me with no time to react—CRASH!

In a state of shock, I immediately got out of my car and rushed to the driver yelling, "Are you okay? Are you okay?" As I came near the vehicle and saw the driver, panic seized me. There was nothing I could do for her and, in hysteria, I ran behind her vehicle and fell on the snowy ground.

I then heard what appeared to be the sound of gushing water and noticed gasoline pouring out from under her car just a few feet from where I sat. As I tried to get up and distance myself, unbearable pain shot through my legs, causing me to collapse and forcing me to drag myself away from her car.

A woman, Joanna, stopped and stayed with me until help arrived. I never saw her face. She stood behind me, keeping me in a sitting position. Joanna wrapped her scarf around my neck and had me put my hands in it to keep them dry and warm.

She kept her hands on my shoulder and spoke softly to calm me down.

I began to pray out loud, "Lord Jesus, please be with her. Protect her, Lord." This was my continuous prayer. When I would stop praying, Joanna would prompt me to keep praying and I continued until the EMTs removed her from the vehicle.

Due to my shock and concern for the other driver, I was unaware of the seriousness of my injuries. When the EMT cut my jeans during transportation to the hospital, it was another shock to see the condition of my legs. I sustained injuries throughout my body that are continuing to appear even as I type this, including head trauma and PTSD from the violent scene of the crash. I can still hear our cars colliding. The dreadful reel of this tragedy plays continually in my mind.

The force of the impact is trapped in my body, heightening my sympathetic nervous system—I am stuck in fight-or-flight. Sounds are louder, everything seems brighter, the nerve endings throughout my body are sensitive to the touch. My mind is filled with confusion as I grapple to maintain a routine. Sometimes I walk in circles, not knowing what I am doing or what day it is. I struggle to come up with ordinary words to complete a sentence. Long naps enable me to reset in order to get through the rest of the day. When traveling to my doctor appointments, I am not at ease, and when I see cars coming in my direction, I brace for impact.

I asked those *why God* questions without even knowing the outcome for the other driver whom I will call Brenda. I wept and pleaded with God for her life. *Lord, heal her. Please heal her.*

My husband contacted my counselor immediately, and we

took steps to guard my mental health, such as not telling me if Brenda passed until I was ready. She was in critical condition and that was all the information I had.

As the days went by, I got the sense that my husband was withholding information from me.

"Did she die?" I asked him six days after the crash.

"No." I believed him, but something wasn't making sense. In two separate conversations, I overheard people asking him, "Did you tell her? Does she know?"

"Then what is it?" I needed to know, but he knew I wasn't ready to receive the news.

All he said was, "Something else happened at the scene." I sat on the couch, confused.

"Something else?" I kept on repeating his statement over and over, then it hit me. "She was pregnant!" I said in a panic.

"Yes," my husband told me.

Brenda lost her baby that day. *"A baby! A baby, God! Oh God, why? I don't understand."* I couldn't process this information at the moment and I still can't. Words cannot express the emotional pain I am holding onto for her and her family.

Life's tragic events often leave us without answers. We cannot make sense of the suffering some people undergo; however, this doesn't change the sovereignty of God. He is still on the throne and in control, even when it hurts.

As the news of the accident spread (we live in a small community), I was afraid someone was going to tell me Brenda didn't make it and catch me off guard. So, about two weeks after the accident, I asked my husband again. "Did she make it?"

"No. She passed."

Even though the accident wasn't my fault, my heart aches. It grieves over lost dreams for Brenda's family. It breaks my heart as a mother who has a son her age, and a daughter that is expecting. I am at a loss for words. Just filled with sorrow.

I felt I had to suffer as Brenda did—something called survivors' guilt—one of those things you have to go through to understand. My left leg was in such rough shape and in so much pain that I figured I deserved to lose it. She lost something; I didn't. I have been battling with obsessive irrational thoughts since this accident.

We can ask many questions when life seems unfair. Did God plan this accident? Why do awful things happen? I have gone down this path and every day have to remind myself to accept that which I cannot change. It isn't easy, and I am not there, yet. Even in the darkest valleys, the Light will get through to me.

The verse I hold on to when hopelessness tries to slither in, when I am in emotional and physical pain, when I am struggling to walk, is the verse I was holding onto in 2020. Same verse, different hardship, still very powerful!

> But he said to me, "My grace is sufficient for you, for my power is made perfect in weakness." Therefore I will boast all the more gladly about my weaknesses, so that Christ's power may rest on me. This is why, for Christ's sake, I delight in weaknesses, in insults, in hardships, in persecutions, in difficulties. For when I am weak, then I am strong. (2 Corinthians 12:9-10)

As for my prayer that morning, asking God to show me the idols in my heart, this is still unfolding. Perhaps I need to keep a check on my relationships and make sure God is above all. Maybe it is time to release my future plans for Fitness Coaching since my body is so broken now. Or possibly I can help a different group of women—those with limitations. I don't know. Right now there is a sense of hopelessness in my life. *Will I ever be physically strong again? Will my brain heal? What about Brenda's family— how are they coping?*

However, what I have really wondered is if Brenda heard my prayers pleading for her life; if she knew Jesus as her Savior? I have wondered if Joanna's beliefs were challenged as she saw me injured, in shock, going to my Father for help. I don't know either of these women's faith journeys. God does. The things that matter most are those that have eternal value. I wonder how much of the small stuff I get wrapped up in and overlook the eternal. What about you?

So now, as I wrestle between unsettled emotions and my heart's desire to bring God glory in my brokenness, my prayer remains—*after some time*, Lord have your will.

A Note From Me

Thank you for picking up this book. It is not by chance that it landed in your hands. I have been praying for you.

If what you've read has blessed you, consider sharing it with a friend and leaving a review where you bought this book, this will enable others to get their hands on it. To make an even bigger impact, lead a group study. Let's reach out to women in our community and assure them they are not alone!

If this book has sparked your interest in writing or exploring your own redemption story, I am currently working on a companion guide. This guide will serve as a tool to draw out your thoughts, memories, and your most cherished stories. It will also encourage you to grow in your faith.

This companion guide offers tried-and-true journaling tips, reflection questions and will challenge you to L.I.V.E. daily as you:

Lean on Jesus.
Invest in Prayer.
Value Others.
Embrace Your Story.

Go to www.solewright.com and sign up for my newsletter to receive this FREE guide once it becomes available. In addition, you'll receive monthly encouragement emails, health tips, updates on future books, and other news from me. I look forward to hearing from you.

L.I.V.E. each day for the glory of God.

> However, as it is written: "What no eye has seen, what no ear has heard, and what no human mind has conceived"—the things God has prepared for those who love him—these are the things God has revealed to us by his Spirit. (1 Corinthians 2:9-10)

Acknowledgements

To my husband, my best friend, who did everything in his power to give me the resources and time to finish this book. Thank you, Duane, for believing in me and not allowing me to quit. I love you.

To my children and their spouses, Brian, Megan, Hannah and Dallas, Jonathan and Alanna, you have been my greatest cheerleaders. Thank you for your support and for encouraging me to share my story. You have my heart.

I want to express my gratitude to the community of women, my sisters in the faith, who have encouraged me, followed up, and those who reviewed this book. Tracy Izatt and Michelle Lyman who were the first to read the rough, un-formatted manuscript. I applaud your patience and endurance in getting through it. Trudy Galla, Stacie Gerathy, and Sallie Krepps, thank you for your feedback and the time you gave to this project.

My friend and graphic designer, Sally Bancroft, you always see what I am thinking.

Rose Canfield you captured the vision of this book. Your input and words of encouragement gave me the push I needed to see this through.

Latisha VanderZon, I could write a whole page about your wisdom, support and editing super powers. I don't know what I would have done without you. Thank you for the time you invested in me and this book.

And to my counselor, Dr. Amy Borgman, wow what a journey! Thank you for your commitment to EMDR and the gift it has offered me.

May God bless you all far more abundantly than what you have blessed me with.

Resources

- Grief Support
  https://www.griefshare.org

- Women's Resource Center
  https://www.womensresourcecenter.org/

- Single Momm
  https://www.singlemomm.org/

- Local Assistance
  https://www.211.org/

- Unplanned Pregnancy
  https://www.heartbeatinternational.org/
  https://www.care-net.org/

- Post abortion
  https://surrenderingthesecret.com/
  https://www.saveone.org/
  https://supportafterabortion.com/
  https://hopeafterabortion.com/
  https://www.hurtafterabortion.com/

- The Abortion Survivors Network
  https://abortionsurvivors.org/

- Substance Abuse
  https://www.celebraterecovery.com/
  https://www.samhsa.gov/

- EMDR
  https://www.emdria.org/

- Suicide hotline 1-888-333-2377 or 988
  Text TALK to 741741
  https://988lifeline.org/
  https://www.crisistextline.org/
  https://afsp.org/
  https://save.org/

- Domestic Abuse Hotline 1-800-799-7233

The website addresses and phone numbers provided are offered as resources to you and are not intended in any way to be or to imply an endorsement by Solé Wright or Sugar Maple Books.

Endnotes

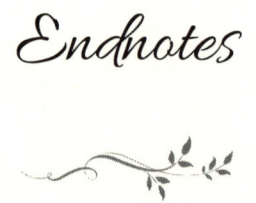

Introduction

    1. Redeemed. https://www.merriam-webster.com/dictionary/redeemed

Chapter 3: Identity

    1. Meaning of Jabez. https://www.biblestudy.org/meaning-names/jabez.html

    2. How Many Verses in the Bible? https://christianityfaq.com/how-many-verses-are-in-the-bible/

    3. Ruby Redfort quotes "Sticks and Stones" Poem: https://www.goodreads.com/quotes/7664736-sticks-and-stones-may-break-my-bones-but-words-can

1. What is an Empath? https://www.verywellmind.com/what-is-an-empath-and-how-do-you-know-if-you-are-one-5119883

2. Ambassador. https://www.merriam-webster.com/dictionary/ambassador accessed 11/28/2022

3. Evans, Tony. Praying Through The Names of God. Harvest House Publishers, 2014.

Chapter 6: Religion or Relationship
1. The Burning Bed. https://www.imdb.com/title/tt0087010/

Chapter 8: Surrender
1. EMDR. https://www.emdria.org/

2. October Baby, directed by Andrew Erwin and John Erwin (Provident Films, 2012), 1:47:00, https://octoberbabymovie.net/

3. Sertell, Robin. Miracles Happen in the Wilderness: A Story of Remembrance. Independent, 2020. https://a.co/d/fVw93Zr

About The Author

Solé Wright is a Certified Fitness Trainer and Lifestyle Wellness Coach who guides women in overcoming personal challenges. She understands the impact of unresolved trauma on personal and spiritual growth. Her approach to health and wellness is to care for the whole person—body, mind, and soul.

After raising four children, she is pursuing her dream of sharing her redemption story and how Jesus has met her on this journey. Solé plans to write another book on releasing negative thought patterns, and has a future project to empower women in writing their own redemption stories.

She enjoys a strong cup of coffee, reading, hiking and taking long walks. Solé and her husband live in Cedar, Michigan, where they dote over their grandchildren.

She wants to hear from her readers. You can message her at sole@solewright.com or visit her website using the qr code.

Made in the USA
Middletown, DE
15 January 2024